An ICT perspective on Private v. Public Healthcare in Canada

George O. Obikoya

Table of Contents

Executive Summary	3
Introduction	6
Public Health Systems Revisited	9
An Analysis of ICT in Health Systems	12
Prospects and Challenges of Private health Systems	28
The Business Value of ICT in Health Systems	46
Conclusions	64
References	66

Executive Summary

Canada s expenditures on both public and private healthcare delivery are substantial, and increasing. Health Care in Canada, a report released by the Canadian Institute for Health Information (CIHI) on June 8, 2005 indicates that Canada spent about $100 billion on healthcare in 2004, about $70 billion and $30 billion of this amount by the public and private health care sectors, respectively. Despite restrictions on the role of private health insurance for publicly insured hospital and physician services, the recent landmark Supreme Court ruling in Chaoulli v. Quebec appears to herald a new epoch in the history of healthcare services in Canada. The ruling, which invalidated the ban on the use of private medical insurance to pay for basic services the public healthcare system offers, on the ground that it violates the Canadian Charter of Rights and Freedoms, reopens the debate over public versus private health system in the country. Indeed, Quebec has initiated moves to comply with the Supreme Court ruling. On November 09, 2005, the province s Premier, Jean Charest indicated at the National Assembly that there was no question that his government would use a notwithstanding law to get around the Supreme Court ruling, which he reiterated was an order, not an invitation. Furthermore, Quebec Health Minister Philippe Couillard plans to introduce a legislative proposal on private care in the Assembly in December 2005 that will establish a parallel private health-care system and allow Quebecers to buy private health insurance for a variety of services currently covered only by public insurance, including hip- and knee-replacement, as early as 2006. It is anathema to some that the country's health system would be anything but publicly funded, and it is unlikely that anyone in Canada would sincerely advocate its replacement with a private health system. Although across the fence, are those convinced that it is only a matter of time before the Supreme Court ruling applies to other Canadian provinces and territories, what most of them advocate is a parallel private health system in the country. Both groups advance numerous reasons for their positions. Supporters of a publicly funded health system argue that it is in keeping with the social contract between Canadians and their government as enshrined in the Canada Health Act. They are concerned that a parallel private health system will create a "two-tiered" health system skewed in favor of those that have the financial resources, and often the political influence to patronize private health insurance. They also contend that a private health system will compromise quality and access to its publicly funded counterpart, for example, luring healthcare professionals, already in short supply, away from the public health system by offering them higher pay. This, they argue could only lengthen, and not shorten hospital waitlists, compromising government efforts to solve this seemingly perennial problem[1].

Advocates of a parallel private health system on the other hand hold that, by lowering government health spending, it guarantees that the public health system remains sustainable. They also claim that by providing an alternative pathway to health services, it will reduce wait times, hence improve access to the public health system, and even enhance its quality by making health systems competitive. A recent Canadian Medical Association (CMA) sponsored Ipsos-Reid survey indicates that most residents of Atlantic Canada, Ontario, Saskatchewan, and Manitoba, and younger adults, and women favor a publicly funded health system, whereas the reverse is true for residents of Alberta, British Columbia, and Quebec, and most Canadians with University education, and those in the higher income brackets[2]. The results of this survey seem to mirror developments past and present in the political and economic arenas in different parts of the country. Pour un Quebec lucide, the manifesto former premier Lucien Bouchard and eleven other Quebec business, media and political elites signed recently warned of the threat to the province's social fabric of its aging workforce, increasing health costs, public debt, and taxes. Also recently, Claude Castonguay, one of the strongest supporters of Medicare in Quebec, expressed similar concerns[3]. Alberta has moved on from the days of the "facility fees" fiasco with Ottawa in the mid-1990s, when it paid up to $7 million per year penalties for the fees private eye surgery clinics charged patients for use of operating theaters, instruments, and other overheads[4]. The province is not now about to give up the over $1 billion the healthcare premiums it charges Albertans contributes to its health budget, nor is it kowtowing to Ottawa or not declaring its preference for a parallel private health systems. Is it surprising that the residents of Saskatchewan, which on September 04, 2005, celebrated its centenary as a Canadian province with, among others, a renewed emphasis on its "gift" of Medicare to Canada, oppose a private health system? Is it also any wonder that the national leader of its ruling party, the New Democratic Party (NDP) recently threatened to defeat the federal government unless it cracked down on private healthcare[6]? The preferences of well-off Canadians vis-à-vis the poor or those of the educated versus the not-so-educated, also reflect the beliefs in certain quarters that only affluent Canadians can afford and therefore will benefit from a parallel health system, leaving a public health system, depleted of its professional cadre and starved of funds to cater for the majority of Canadians. However, leaving these polarized views aside for a moment peel offs the artifacts and reveals the nuances of the issues, including what the extent of government involvement in healthcare provision should be, how much competition, market forces, and effective regulation influence it, and the factors that enhance, or compromise performance in public and private health systems, both inherently flawed anyway.

The issues involved with the choice of health system for Canada are many and complex. This paper examines some of these issues. It discusses the merits and demerits of public and private health systems, and analyzes opposing views of the debate. For example, the paper examines the effectiveness of the current health system and its challenges, if a parallel private healthcare system would be more effective in reducing wait times, and the overall costs of running a public versus a private health system. It also examines broader views regarding the interplay of political, social, economic, and technology forces in the success or otherwise of any health system, including in the financial rearrangement, insurance regulation and risk, and other issues that a shift to a private health system would engender. Private healthcare programs have always complemented Canada s public health system, covering the supplemental services that fall outside the basic health care coverage the latter provides. Even this traditional cooperation is increasingly untenable, with provincial health spending soaring, and private health plans having to provide more coverage for example, as some provinces de-insure certain healthcare coverage, hence bear more costs, both groups thus forced back to the drawing table to redefine their strategies. There is hardly any disputing that Canada's health system is at the precipice of change. The issues involved with the choice of health system for Canada are indeed, legion, and intricate, an exploration of which is an essential path of what is likely to be an ongoing evolution of the country's health system. This is an important point as the tone of the current debate suggests a final resolution, that settling for one or the other health system is an end in itself. Whereas, regardless of which system eventually emerges, it will undergo continuous monitoring and evaluation of its performance, and will be subject to change if necessary. It may be poignant at the juncture to ask what role information and communications technologies (ICT) could play in this transition process and indeed, in charting the future path of Canada s health system. The question may sound odd but it is not entirely out of place considering the results a province such as Saskatchewan has been able to achieve regarding solving its wait lists problem, a remarkable 3,200 decrease of its surgical waitlists in 2005 compared to the previous year, according to data recently released by the province s Surgical Care Network. By simply publishing its waitlists on the Internet, the province provided information that not only helped patients, but also doctors to make informed decisions about treatment options, and the province to optimize scarce professional workforce and hospital resources. Should the question then not be how much more ICT could do to help solve some of the problems that triggered the call for a parallel private health system in the first place, or make the public health system more cost-effective and competitive, and as some would argue, perhaps even make the public v private health system debate immaterial?

Introduction

T he Canada Health Act (CHA or the Act), Canada s federal law for publicly funded health care insurance, governs public health care, whose design is to provide all eligible persons in Canada with prepaid, comprehensive, and accessible insured health services, with no direct charges where individuals receive health services. Because the Act is a sort of covenant between Canadians and their government, it also ensures consistency of healthcare delivery across the country, even though each province or territory runs its health services. The onus then is on the federal government to enforce the letter and spirit of the Act, which it attempts to do by making its health funds transfers to the provinces and territories on certain conditions and terms, specifically that health care must be: comprehensive, portal, universal, accessible, and be publicly administered free for insured services. These are the Five principles of Canada Health Act, which according to Romanow[7] ..began as simple conditions attached to federal funding for

Medicare. Over time, they became much more than that. Today, they represent both the values underlying the health care system and the conditions that governments attach to funding a national system of public health care. The principles have stood the test of time and continue to reflect the values of Canadians." Romanow was Premier of Saskatchewan between 1991 and 2001. He headed the Commission on the Future of Healthcare in Canada established on April 04, 2001 by former Prime Minister Jean Chrétien, the Commission's report, released in 2002.

The Act sets out the primary objective of Canadian health care policy, which is *to protect, promote, and restore the physical and mental well-being of residents of Canada, and to facilitate reasonable access to health services without financial or other barriers* [7]. It seems therefore reasonable to assume that without any substantive changes to The Act, the country's health policy must aim to meet the requirements of The Act, which would be in keeping with the expectations of Canadians. These are appropriate starting points for an examination of which of private or public health insurance suits Canada better at this point in the country's history. In order to conduct a thorough and objective examination, it would be also be appropriate to ask if the public health system currently in place achieving the objectives of The Act, and if not, would a private health system do so, or would both systems operating in tandem be the best approach to satisfying the requirements of the Act? Clearly, the answers to these questions would not come at the snap of the fingers. Indeed, it would require answers to several other questions to lie bare the effectiveness and efficiency of the current public health system, and its weaknesses, vis-à-vis the prospects and challenges of a private or a hybrid health system.

What exactly is the status of the Canada Health Act? Is the Act enforceable, and if so, enforced? Some provinces, for examples Saskatchewan and British Columbia, have provincial health legislation that complement and enforce the Canada Health Act, others do not, and yet others, such as Nova Scotia, are in the process of enacting such laws. Examples of these provincial laws include prohibition of extra billing for materials or facilities, and ensuring that doctors that no longer operate under the insured system do not charge more than what the government would pay for the services were they operating in the insured system. Ontario's Bill 8 of June 2004, for example among others establishes the Ontario Health Quality Council to monitor the province's health system. The Bill also aims to prevent wait-list queue skipping, and extra billing, and to promote accountability among health care providers. Every province and territory in Canada is obliged to run its health services in accordance with the provisions of the Canada Health Act, even without these complementary laws. However, critics are quick to point out indications of violations of these provisions, particularly with regard to healthcare providers operating outside the provincial/ territorial health system. The number of private, for-profit clinics and hospitals in Quebec, for example, has been increasing steadily, even before Chaoulli v. Quebec, creating opportunities for those with the financial resources to seek private healthcare and avoid queuing for services in the public health system, which they stress directly contravenes the universality principle of the Canada Health Act. There are other examples of alleged violations of the principles the Act in other provinces/ territories, for extra billing for facilities, in direct contravention to its accessibility principle. To counter these charges, others argue that private healthcare is an integral part of Canada's health system anyway since public health insurance does not cover certain healthcare costs, such as the dentist's or optometrist's bill, or that for a private hospital bed, or even ambulance fees. Each person has to pay for these services via his or her employer, or extended health insurance coverage, or in cash, but Canadians are ever paying even more for private healthcare insurance, its opponents would again posit.

Some even insist that the Act is not enforceable. They buttress their claim with the examples of certain private healthcare institutions that existed before the Canada Health Act of 1984, the Medical Care Act of 1968, even the Hospital Insurance and Diagnostic Services Act of 1957, which continue to operate even now. Medicare covers some of their services, but not others. The Shouldice Hospital in Toronto, established in 1945, and renowned for hernia repairs, but whose services only Ontario residents enjoy under Medicare, is one such institution. There are other for-profit clinics and hospitals in the country, and many private computerized tomography (CT) scan, magnetic resonance imaging (MRI), and other diagnostic centers all over Canada, some on provincial government contracts and aimed to reduce wait times, doctors in some cases paid on a fee-for-service basis, others strictly privately run, in either case the centers, run for profit. Many see these arrangements as clear violations of the Act, including the current Liberal government, which signaled its intention to stamp out private healthcare, once in office in 2003. Others consider the government's plan unnecessary, and in fact, counterproductive, arguing that private healthcare actually helps achieve the goals of the Act, for example, shortening wait lists. They also contend that doctors will actually end up remaining in the public system if part of their practice could become private and they are not solely dependent on government's payment scheme. For yet others, that the Act is the law is not negotiable, and reasons adduced to justify its violation simply unsound. They point to Canadians disillusionment with their health services as a clear indication of the need to comply with the provisions of the Act. An Ipso-Reid surveys conducted in July 2005, and sponsored by the CMA showed that Canadians were unimpressed by their healthcare system since 2003, nor thought it would improve in future. They also thought that they had overrated their health system compared to those of other Organization for Economic Cooperation and Development (OECD) countries. Sixty-three percent of Canadians gave the health system a B grade or better, same score as in 2004, and 50% felt that it would get somewhat (36%), or much worse (14%) over the next two to three years, a less optimistic view, actually a 13-point rise over the percentage of Canadians that felt the same way, in 2003. The survey also showed that Canadians correctly rated their country 8_{th} out 30 among OECD countries regarding life expectancy, but not in terms of performance indicators including how much of its health system is publicly funded, the number of doctors per person, and how much of their money they paid for healthcare. Is it counter-intuitive to conclude that these findings could rally support for calls for improving the country's health system?

Public health systems revisited

Canada has always had an enviable public health system, on which, however, it spends a

significant portion of its Gross Domestic Product (GDP), 10.1% in 2004. According to 2002 comparative figures, the latest available, Canada at 9.6% is fourth among G8 countries in total health expenditure as a percentage of GDP, after the United States (14.6%), Germany (10.9%) and France (9.7%), with the UK, Italy, Japan and Russia, next in that order. Indeed, Canada plans to spend $41 billion on its health system over the next decade, with an additional $805 million over the next five fiscal years. Just less then 30% of the country s health expenditures funds hospital and drugs. Projections indicate that the overall health spending will continue to increase for some time to come, a main source of concern for not only the government but also Canadians. In 1996, the country s public health expenditures were $75.2 billion, and $95.1 billion in 2000, a 26% increase, and projected to increase as a share of total provincial and territorial government revenues from 31% in 2000 to 42% by 2020, annual average public, and private health costs projected to increase by 5.2% and 5.0%, respectively, over the same period9. Projected increase in per capita spending adjusted for inflation for the same period were 58% and 17% for healthcare, and all other government spending, respectively9. What more does anyone need to realize the need for revisiting the funding and structure of the Canadian health system some would holler? Indeed, some may suggest that the fact that the public sector is bereft of competition compounds its tenuous capacity to deliver the goods not only in terms of the often-obvious structural limitations in its workforce, but also a lack of managerial autonomy, which its apologists may attribute to the socio-political milieu in which it operates. Canada is certainly not averse to health reforms. Indeed, it is an ongoing process in the country, the federal government infusing $16 billion into its Health Reform Fund only two years ago. The question is the extent to which it has implemented and plans to implement the classical dimensions of this exercise, particularly healthcare financing, for example via non-tax revenue sources, with which incidentally, even some countries, such as the UK that have implemented far-reaching health reform programs, have resisted tinkering.

It is arguable whether a parallel private health system will solve all of Canada s healthcare delivery woes, and uncertain that the continued involvement of government in healthcare delivery is the panacea for the frailties of market forces. What is not disputable is the need for the public health system to find ways to contain skyrocketing health costs, yet deliver qualitative healthcare. Clearly, there is no one-way to do this but there is also little doubt that investments in appropriate ICT to achieve strategic healthcare objectives will help streamline operations, facilitate effective and qualitative healthcare delivery, and reduce costs. Clinical decision support alerts and reminders can help reduce service use by reducing adverse drug events, rationalizing drug prescribing, offering options to costly medications, and reducing orders for laboratory and radiology tests. As far back as 1994, The UK Audit Commission estimated that the country could save £ 425m annually on prescribing in general practice in England and Wales by complying to simple rules such as a reminder system could promote, for examples, increasing prescription of generic drugs, and decreasing prescription of ineffective drugs[10]. Decision support systems (DSS) and a variety of other ICT also help improve care and patient safety, enable universality of care, enhance its comprehensiveness, increase accessibility to care, reduce hospitalization rates, and ultimately reduce costs. A 2003 cost-benefit analysis of electronic medical records use by primary care physicians in an ambulatory setting showed a 5-year net benefit per provider of US$86,400, the results of a five-way sensitivity analysis with the most pessimistic and optimistic assumptions, ranging from a US$2300 net cost to a US$330,900 net benefit[11]. Healthcare providers in Canada could save substantially, even accrue revenues, from the averted costs of paper charts pulls, re-filings, and transcriptions and the governments even more from implementing electronic health records (EHR.). Computerized physician order entry (CPOE) alone, in addition to ensuring patient safety, reducing medical errors, according to some studies by over 50%, flagging redundant laboratory tests, and offering options for less expensive drugs, saved Brigham and Women s Hospital, in Boston, Mass., upwards of $10 million, since it went live on October 07, 2002[12]. How much could Canada, with most of its health expenditures spent on hospitals and drugs save if its hospitals implemented CPOE, not mention the many lives this could save and the improved quality of care delivered?

Not only the clinical domains benefit from health ICT implementation, other components of the health sector also do, as the November 2001 report of a task Force on supply chain management initiated jointly by the Ontario Hospital Association (OHA) and the Efficient Healthcare Consumer Response (EHCR), show. The report notes that it costs Ontario hospitals approximately $250 million annually to handle and process Ontario s health care supplies, and that implementing supply chain IT and best practices could reduce these costs, at least, by 15%, or about $40 million. Furthermore, implementing best practices would reduce overall costs of supplies by a minimum of 5%, or $80 million, a total savings to Ontario hospitals of about $120 million per year, and considering that Ontario is about a third of the Canadian market, total annual savings across Canada of about $350 million. There are many more examples of the costs savings and other benefits of health ICT in different health sectors[13].

Even in a developed country such as Canada with a highly literate populace, hence, with no major informational asymmetry between health provider and patient, ICT remains the bedrock of public health services, to which the government's ICT investments in its ongoing primary care reforms attest. ICT is also crucial to service delivery at other levels of the health system. Furthermore, and even with a parallel private health system in situ, not only may there still be the need for regulating private health insurance, one cannot dismiss historical and political antecedents in any consideration of the nature and extent of government health financing. This is more so in the context of the existing institutions in the country, their capabilities, and how they interact with one another, continuing investments in whose underlying ICT fabric create an enabling environment for responsibility, accountability, consumer empowerment, and dynamic capacity-building. By fostering collaboration among these institutions, ICT also minimizes the negative impact the information lop-sidedness that the silo-like services in top-down health systems often engenders, not least on policy implementation. Coupled with facilitating such measures as the providing stronger incentives for excellent performance and promoting public sector quasi-market milieus, apposite ICT investments in the public health system may indeed, improve the quality of its services sufficiently to nullify any perceived advantage of a parallel private health system, and make the public v private healthcare debate redundant. It may therefore, be necessary to revisit the crucial part ICT could play in defining the appropriate role of government in healthcare delivery in Canada, particularly in striking the right balance between direct service provision and policy-making.

An Analysis of ICT in Health Systems

State-funded healthcare has been under siege for a long time. In England for example, where it started over four centuries ago, when elderly and ill in society received care from religious orders in monasteries, it fizzled with their dissolution at the excommunication of King Henry VIII by the Pope following his establishment of the Church of England in a bid to legitimize his second marriage to Anne Boleyn[14]. England did not totally abandon its most needy, and in 1601, Queen Elizabeth I enacted the first *Poor Law* to cater for them, but the almshouses subsequently established lost public favor in the C19th because they were allegedly too benevolent, the poor, elderly, and infirm moved into more austere workhouses. Improved knowledge of disease pathology led to the development of a variety of services and the separation of these peoples, with for examples, infectious diseases hospitals, primary and community care services, and institutions for the mentally handicapped established. By the beginning of the C20th, government funded insurance schemes that supported the burgeoning family doctor service, Lloyd George, the British Prime Minister extending the scheme to all workers who chose from a panel of General Practitioners (GP). The scheme termed, the Panel System although did not cover the men s families, many poor people were able to obtain free health services. The idea of a comprehensive, state-funded, health service was already coming together prior to World War II with the establishment of an Emergency Medical Service in 1938. It crystallized with the establishment of the National Health Service (NHS) ten years later by the new labor government, making it the first time a UK government became fully responsible for providing such services to the country s entire populace. The NHS has since then undergone a series of reforms in part driven by the need to better manage and integrate the centrally funded, health service tripod, namely state-owned hospitals, a national GP network, and community/ domiciliary services, each trunk reflecting the diverse origins of the health services. Only lately, did the NHS provide within it and commission all three trunks, but even then, local and central government still control personal social services, long-term elderly care, and housing, environment, and other services indispensable to health[14].

Some form of private health service has always existed in the U.K, despite that the British have mostly received free health services since the establishment of the NHS. Furthermore, the NHS split doctors into two groups; salaried employees, comprising hospital specialists and trainee doctors and; independent contractors, made up of GPs and most dentists. Hospital doctors with part-time NHS contracts could seek private sector employment, which some contend compromised rational utilization of healthcare professionals, and even created a tense milieu of intra and inter-professional power play, essentially every reform effort to rectify these anomalies coming to naught, until recently. What could Canada learn from the UK experiences regarding these anomalies, for example, with regard to the issue of wait times, now and in particular if the country eventually ran a parallel private health system? One of the reasons opponents of the parallel health system adduce is that it would deplete the public health system of scarce health professionals, who would likely seek higher pays in the private health system. As happened in the U.K, even if governments in Canada permitted its doctors did part-time in the private health system, as already is the case in some provinces, in a bid for example to prevent losing its entire health professional workforce to the private health sector, would it not compromise healthcare delivery in the public system? Worse still, how would it affect the current debate on whether wait times benchmarks should be national, the position that the Canadian Medical Association and Canada Health endorse, or as some contend, because of the disparities in the doctor/ patient ratios in different parts of the country, provincial/ territorial? Some even ponder the correct interpretation of the first set of evidence-based medically acceptable wait times and other phrases as contained in the communiqué the country's Health Ministers issued after their October 2005 meeting to determine the standards for wait times they expect the provinces/ territories to deliver by the end of 2005. Granted there could be scientific evidence for particular complications to arise if particular patients suffering from some specific disorder did not receive some particular treatment within a particular time frame, does this statement itself not indicate the complexity of implementing wait times benchmarks some would ask?

The fluidity of research evidence would further complicate this benchmark, not to mention the difficulties implementing the standards were the healthcare professionals simply not there, others would contend, even ask how a parallel health system would not further skew healthcare professionals distribution, making it even more difficult to implement wait times benchmarks, at least in the public health sector. Having said this however, would anyone argue that the lives of some Canadians are less valuable than of others, which is what to which having differential wait-time yardsticks are essentially tantamount? How does it sound that a province knowing the facts about how long people could wait for cancer treatment for example, before they stood significant risks of losing their lives due to complications of the disease, established a longer wait-time standard, just because it has fewer doctors per 1000 people than another province that instituted the appropriate standard? Is it any wonder then that the CMA and Health Canada hold the position that they do? In any case, is it only the number of doctors in a province or territory that determines how long people wait for health services? If so, how did Saskatchewan, with only 1093 general practitioners and 403 specialists in 2005, reduce its wait lists by 3,200 in 2005 compared to 2004, according to data recently released by the province s Surgical Care Network? The Fraser Institute, the Vancouver-based research organization on October 18, 2005 released its annual survey of average waiting times for medical treatment in Canada. This survey showed that the total waiting time for patients between referral from a GP and treatment decreased to 17.7 weeks in 2005 from 17.9 weeks in 2004 across the country. The survey also showed that Saskatchewan people waited, on average, 7.8 fewer weeks for treatment. If the average wait-time in Saskatchewan based on the Surgical Care Network estimates 14 or 15 weeks were correct, and not the 25.5 weeks by the Fraser Institute survey, it is less than the 16.3 weeks average for Ontario, with 10,545 generalists and 8,415 specialists in 2005. The Fraser survey says Ontario has the shortest average wait times in the country, the Saskatchewan authorities think different. However, there is no dispute regarding the significant drop in wait times in Saskatchewan, which the pioneering efforts of the province in publishing its wait lists on an Internet website helped achieve. This information improves informed decision-making about treatment and testing options by patients and doctors, hence help optimize scarce professional work force, and hospital resources. Would the province have been able to achieve this feat setting a lower standard as its goal or with doctors insisting they would not refer patients to a specialist that they did not know, with some specialists ending up with a long wait-list while other sit idly in their offices? Should information on doctors working in a province not be readily available to the public as in Manitoba, which has a Family Doctor Connection phone line program? Extended to include specialists lists, would such lists not enable the public know the family doctors accepting new patients, and allay the fears of some doctors and even patients regarding referrals? Further, with a parallel private health system in place, would government be prescribing a different higher or lower wait times standards for the private health sector? These issues appear to be important for consideration not just to improve the public health system now, but also to prepare it for survival, in case the country eventually has a parallel private health system, and to determine regulatory and policy guidelines for different aspects of running a parallel private health system. Importantly also, should governments not be taking a closer look at what ICT could achieve in terms of solving the wait lists, and other nagging policy, and operational issues in the health system?

Some of the difficulties in the way in reforming the U.K health system included the hierarchical management structure of the hospitals, and largely the community services, which latter though the local governments ran, as opposed to the less rigid management of the GPs, who were independent contractors, via a national contract of services. Another problem was the lack of accountability that the tripartite hospital management by a medical superintendent, matron, and lay administrator created, and there were the problems emanating from the then practice of historical budgeting, due for example to being unrelated to population size or need. The 1974 reorganization of the NHS made some headway, including pushing the concept of population-based health funding further ahead, and harmonizing the management of health services within geographic boundaries, which brought into being the Regional Health Boards under the new Area Health Authorities, themselves under Management Boards comprising lay citizens who the Secretary of State for Health appointed. Significantly and despite its successes, the 1974 reforms could not eliminate historical budgeting, proved to be laden with managers, many redundant, and was overly bureaucratic. These problems continued to be central in the 1980s reform efforts, and Sir Roy Griffiths in his 1984 report, sponsored by the UK government at the time, attempted to solve them with a number of wide-ranging recommendations[15]. The highlight of his report was the replacement of consensus with the more flexible and leadership-oriented, general management approach. This was a paradigm shift, which contradicted the views of an earlier Royal Commission with operational units within health districts allotted budgets for their entire operations rather than for individual functions such as transport, catering, supply, and so on. The increasing use of financial information systems at the time, which facilitated the allocation of costs to clinical activities, and the subsequent introduction clinically-based budgeting and management information systems, played major roles and indeed, brought clinical specialty-level based cost allocation to the fore, and heralded the new business-oriented approach to healthcare management that matured over the years. Canada is one of the many developed countries that subscribe to current public sector management principles sometimes referred to as "New Public Management" (NPM), whose main thrust the direction health services management in the UK typifies. However, it remains uncertain, although many would say doubtful that Canada will carry the reform elements of this management approach to the extent that the UK has, which is to privatize it health services, even if partly.

Many contend somewhat derisively that the healthcare industry, despite being one of the most information-intensive, lags behind other such industries significantly, according to some estimates by as many as a decade, in the use of ICT . This is true to a large extent but it is also noteworthy that the healthcare industry has been using financial management systems for well over two decades. Indeed, as the U.K health reforms show, the use of management information systems helped revolutionize the country's health system and move it further towards business-style management and away from the top-heavy hierarchical management approach of yore that was weighed down with many, albeit avoidable problems. The modest successes of these reform efforts emboldened successive U.K governments to forge ahead with open-market health reforms, even if only contextually, and no doubt attest to how ICT could facilitate the achievement of health policies and reforms. ICT continues to play that role, worldwide today, particularly in the developed world, including Canada. The issue of a parallel health system in Canada introduces a number of different dimensions to the role information systems would play in healthcare delivery in Canada in such dispensation. One reason critics of the private health system denounce it is the fear that it would compromise the public health system. It is reasonable to assume that any private health system is essentially going to be business-oriented, which inherently buttresses this fear. In other words, one could expect healthcare providers operating in the private health system to seek profitability, which suggests that they will use all the means that they could to achieve this goal, one likely to be harder to achieve in the competitive milieu in which they will operate. One of the first things healthcare providers in the private health system will likely do in order to outperform competition is to recruit a corps of highly qualified professionals, and wherefrom than the available pool in the country, at least before looking elsewhere. Technology will likely be the next major differentiating factor, private healthcare providers scrambling to populate their client base by offering hi-tech services and facilities. ICT already in relatively common use in the administrative, and financial services in the health sector will unlikely differentiate one healthcare provider from another, although will continue to feature prominently in these establishments, albeit with vendors competing in what amounts to a mature market, which is not going to be easy. The recognition by these healthcare providers of the need for innovative technologies for any differentiation to occur will stimulate research and development (R&D) in software and IT firms that would mutually benefit the firms and the healthcare providers. The extent to which the public health system will be able to match the private health system in this regard remains conjectural, but likely minimal, at least considering the probable direction of their respective interests regarding potentially valuable technologies. Indeed, would this divergence of interests have any bearing on either system, or the relationship between them? Rather than be seen as competing one with another, should we not be seeing each as having different roles to play in healthcare delivery in the country, roles a reappraisal of the influence of ICT on both systems could help clarify? If the private health system focused its attention on technologies that directly relate to service delivery, should the public system be competing with its private health counterpart, or should it be investing in ICT directed at fortifying population health, for example? The point is not that the public health system should stock dated technologies. Far from that, it should have modern technologies. However, it needs not be in the race to outsmart the private health system investing huge sums of money developing highly specialized, high-end software or equipment, which the private health providers would need to do at in order to thrash their competition.

Arguably, the most controversial of the UK health reforms was the so-called internal market introduced in 1989, whose main goal was to produce a more responsive and efficient health service by promoting a competitive milieu. The British government was keen to align service provision with existing resources, but many argue that the seeming efficiency gains vis-à-vis transaction costs were fake, due largely to factors such as improved data and information capture and medical technologies, and modes of healthcare delivery. Some even contend that the healthcare market is too flawed for genuine competition to occur, and that as evident in the U.S, competition could end up increasing costs as providers broaden service scope so that they could obtain contracts, akin to what the fee-for-service payment scheme for doctors allegedly does to health costs in Canada. They might have rationalized the health service via hospital closures, saving costs, but did these reforms ensure equity, and what about the many bilateral purchasers/ providers monopolies they spun others would ask? Some would even assert that the case of the U.K highlights the need for government to be wary about being embroiled in market-based, healthcare delivery, and rather to focus more on policy formulation that will not only define the extent of its service provision but also its regulatory duties, particularly in relation to the private health sector. For example, should government not be more concerned with what additional or revised health services Medicare should cover in the event of a parallel private health system coming into being, and with the nature and extent of its regulations in a bid to ensure a working overall health system, and to ensure accountability, good governance, and equity? Concerning ICT, for example, would it not help the country to improve the overall health of its citizens investing on Canada Health Infoway (CHI) than on individual technologies with much narrower utilities? Would government not only then need to worry about how to incorporate the private health system into this veritable patient information resource, including establishing policies on confidentiality and security of patient and other information, a situation similar to which the U.S government had to confront recently? The U.S Department of Health and Human Services (HHS) on October 06, 2005, announced two proposed regulations to eliminate legal barriers preventing healthcare providers and organizations from sharing patient information with physicians in a move to facilitate the adoption of electronic prescribing tools and electronic health records (EHR.) It also established a certification group set up to ensure systems interoperability and seamless data and information sharing. In a related move, the Centers for Medicare and Medicaid Services announced its plans for initiating e-prescribing standards binding all Medicare prescription drug plans with the commencement of the Medicare drug benefit in January 2006, and for making exceptions to the "physician self-referral, or Stark Amendment. Doctors in the U.S who participate in Medicare cannot presently refer Medicare patients to hospitals or other healthcare providers with which they have financial dealings. HHS Office of Inspector General has also proposed protection from a federal anti-kickback statute, which would permit donations of e prescribing and EHR technology to doctors, provided these gifts meet requisite certification guidelines. Such efforts to find the right balance between consumer protection and health ICT diffusion will also likely be ongoing concerns for Canadian governments whether or not a parallel private health system exists.

With private healthcare providers focusing on technologies based on their need to attract patients and outperform one another, should government not focus on technologies that will enhance access to care by its citizens that cannot afford private healthcare, or live in unreachable areas and on remote farms? Should government not be keener on implementing technologies that will bolster primary care, and those that will contain overall health spending, and do these considerations interest private health providers largely? One reason some claim that the U.S health system is expensive, problematic and needs fixing is that major hospitals and healthcare providers have gone beyond the care levels most patients need, focusing on complex and esoteric diseases, and ignoring commoner disorders for which most people seek treatment[16], hence the suggestion for more attention to developing disruptive technologies. These technologies, which are simpler, and more affordable and expedient products and services, proponents argue, will facilitate more broad-based service provision in affordable settings. Think of angioplasty, which replaced expensive and complicated open-heart surgeries, and its impact on costs. Does it not underscore the need for government to focus on technologies that will improve the quality of health of and of healthcare delivery to all Canadians? Indeed, such a focus on disruptive technologies will unlikely harm the private health sector, which individuals seeking more exclusive treatment approaches will likely still patronize, nor will it hurt software and ICT vendors who will probably, on the contrary, be opening up new markets with robust prospects of making profits, with each innovative disruptive technology that they develop. There is no gainsaying that governments will benefit just as much investing research and development (R&D) funds on such technologies and encouraging its healthcare providers to use them and patients to embrace them. It seems apt therefore to suggest that governments shun high-end ICT and invest in and monitor usage of software and ICT that will facilitate accurate diagnosis and ensure appropriate treatment, particularly of the commoner diseases, by pairing practitioners' knowledge and skills with the complexity of the medical case they handle, and enabling referral to appropriate professional level and or specialty. This, no doubt will reduce wait times, morbidity, and mortality rates, and obviate the need for needless lab and diagnostic investigations and drug treatments, hence reduce overall health costs in lives, productivity, and health spending. Since most private health systems will likely have other concerns besides reducing wait times, it may be more meaningful, from a financial standpoint, for them to focus on esoteric technologies for specialized care, in sophisticated, highly specialized cardiac treatment centers, for example. Thus, government may fare better financially focusing less on establishing such facilities, but more on all-purpose general hospitals.

Furthermore, should government not be paying closer attention to its role in minimizing the consequences of healthcare market imperfections on its citizens, particularly the poor? Is this the more urgent with some provinces shedding their Medicare commitments, hence private health insurers taking on more services, and employers, and individuals paying the bills if Canada were to prevent the sort of health insurance crisis at General Motors in the USA, likely related to the eventual firing of 30,000 employees in November 2005? That the two health systems have disparate priorities calls the fears of protagonists on either side into question. What it does not dispute is the need for each health system to pursue its stated objectives with remarkable vigor, and ICT is going to play a crucial role in this regard. It is also pertinent to note that the factors that operate in a competitive market environment could be quite harsh. This may be a new reality for doctors, many not accustomed to the often-vicious market forces they will encounter, for examples, mergers, acquisitions, and hostile takeovers. These forces may scare some doctors away from the private health system or force them out, and back into the public health system, but some others to reap the benefits of overwhelming entry barriers, and other competitive forces, which again, make one wonder if the perceived fear of exodus of healthcare professionals to the private health system is not overblown.

The public versus parallel private health system debate becomes even more complex in relation to the interactions between them, in particular regarding questions about whether government should purchase health services, and what such services should be from the private sector. This interface between public and private health systems highlights the ongoing health reform issues that governments in the country must address. Even presently, government buys services from private health services providers in some Canadian provinces, particularly diagnostic services. The 1989 reforms in the U.K created furor in some quarters despite its noble intentions. The business orientation and competition they fostered sounded good to some but others saw the reforms, implemented in 1991 as privatizing the health services and driving a wedge between NHS institutions. Further, what some perceived as the freedom of the Trusts to purchase the best services based on the needs of the population they served, others, particularly fund-holding GPs saw as siring purchaser/ provider behemoths. Many fund-holding GPs were also displeased with restrictions on the hospital and diagnostic services they could purchase and non-fund-holding GPs viewed contracting of health services as against the freedom of their patients to choose hospitals to which their GPs referred them, resulting in many GPs opting for fund-holding status to secure that freedom. Whether health reforms in Canada will ever get to the point of establishing such Trusts is doubtful. Nor is the country likely to have fund-holding GPs that use government funds to buy health services for their patients, regardless how sound the idea being to make hospitals more competition-oriented hence improve their services, and to trim down wait lists is. The current primary care reforms in Canada aim to strengthen the usual entry-point of the pathways to healthcare. Primary care physicians in Canada also play a significant role in reducing wait lists. However, it seems much has to do with approaches to remuneration for this to happen, although preferential referral is another key issue, with many GPs not referring patients to specialists they do not know, even if the option is for the patient to join the queue on their preferred specialist's long wait lists. Some are quick to say that many doctors support private healthcare because of their pecuniary interests but the issues involved are much more profound than just wage hikes. There is no dispute on the link between performance and reward in fostering improved output quality, yet there is little agreement on which of capitation (weighted population basis), apparently preferred by most Canadian doctors, fee-for-service, which has lately received a lot of negative publicity, or something in between, is the best way to remunerate doctors. The reform of provider payment system is nonetheless, one of the first reforms governments must address in order to promote job fulfillment, enhance productivity, and foster competition, and to ensure equity and accessibility and overall, to improve the quality of healthcare Canadians receive. Engaging in this exercise will therefore enable the Canadian government to move health service delivery closer toward a business-like orientation, with its associated improvements in efficiency and effectiveness, without necessarily privatizing its health services.

GPs in Canada do not have a budget to purchase services for their patients, but health regions, representing provincial governments, health insurers, usually private for-profit enterprises, and employers, do, and Canadians are increasingly using more of their own money to purchases health services too. In other words, the health system in Canada, although embraces many of the principles regarding business-style management, is in principle, publicly funded, and although elements of privatization exist, it is not as privatized as the U.K health system. The issue at stake is not that of Canada privatizing its health system but enabling whoever chooses to seek services that Medicare normally covers, from private health services, which, with a few exceptions, do not currently have legal authority to provide such services. Nonetheless, many would agree that governments in the country ought to start looking at their options now just in case court rulings in the future mandate them to legalize private health system, as it already did in Quebec. Even now, many provincial and territorial governments find themselves in a bind regarding whether to build or buy services, for example to implement magnetic resonance imaging services in a remote hospital serving a limited number of individuals when a major center offering these services exists a few miles away although across the country's border. Even assuming that Canada runs a private health system, deciding whether to purchase the services from a private healthcare provider not far off could also pose a dilemma except policy guidelines exist. Although applying basic principles of transaction costs could help in making such a decision, that is, to build if high, and buy, if low, one must not underrate political and other extraneous factors that could come into play in making such decisions, which is why considerations of such issues should not wait until court rulings. Governments will certainly be keen to lower transaction costs of ICT for example, as part of its overall bid to reduce health spending, while simultaneously reaping the benefits of health ICT purchased at minimal costs. The Canadian federal government recently committed a $46 million investment, and that of Ontario, the latter through the Ontario Automotive Investment Strategy recently committed $46 million, and $76.8 million, respectively to support the $768 million investment of DaimlerChrysler Canada Inc. (DCCI) in its Windsor and Brampton, Ontario operations, investments critical to ensuring the industry's competitiveness in the global market. This is according to The Honorable David L. Emerson, federal Minister of Industry, and the Honorable Joseph Cordiano, Ontario Minister of Economic Development and Trade, in an announcement on November 21, 2005. The funds will support innovations and flexibility in manufacturing processes, and R&D in collaboration with the University of Windsor. This is the sort of initiative that governments at the federal and provincial/territorial levels should also be supporting in the health sector, particularly with respect to developing disruptive technologies, which should help reduce overall health spending by reducing transactions costs, incidentally a significant proportion of the Gross National Product (GNP) in Canada and indeed, other developed countries presently.

The argument for using transaction costs ties in with what governments decisions on the best ways to intervene in mitigating the adverse consequences of market flaws in the event of a parallel health system existing in the country should be. For example, should government decide to subsidize expensive, high-transaction costs health services that it must purchase, for less financially endowed Canadians? If so, how should it do that? Should it be via a special government-sponsored health insurance for affected individuals and in affected areas, with audit and regulatory processes in situ to minimize its abuse, or should it be via health vouchers, or some other mechanisms? What other kinds of services would government need to purchase from the private health sector, why, and how much should transaction costs feature in such decisions, assuming it may have to purchase some essential services despite high transaction costs? Governments need to give such issues early considerations in anticipation of the country not being able to prevent the emergence of a parallel private health system in the end. With regard to regulation, which is an important aspect of accountability, another key reform issue, government has to weigh when to play that role, and when it should cede it to another organization, for example, a professional organization, for which it may be easier to monitor, and ensure compliance with standard professional and ethical practice. This is in keeping with the tenets of the principal-agent dynamics in institutional reforms. It also underscores the need for government to liaison with professional associations such as the Canadian Medical Association, and institutions such as the Colleges of Physicians and Surgeons throughout the country. It is more appropriate and likely easier for these bodies to relate to doctors on such matters as encouraging them to adopt ICT, prior to government instituting regulations and legislation on ICT use, for example. This is more so considering that there is little doubt regarding the likelihood of continuing reviews of such regulations on issues such as privacy, confidentiality, security, governance, and reporting issues, which governments will have to do at some point in keeping with changing times, and which will be binding on doctors and other healthcare professionals.

The fact is that times are changing so fast that government needs to adopt new strategies for tackling the emerging realities of the health of Canadians in order to fulfill its health mandate to them. These changes are both internal and external to the country. Internal changes for examples include ageing of the population, the increasing prevalence of substance use and associated disorders, including the spread of infectious diseases such as Hepatitis C and HIV, the rising rates of chronic diseases such as Diabetes and heart diseases, and the shortage of healthcare professionals, aggravated by the rising numbers of retiring doctors, among others. External influences include the looming threat of avian flu pandemic, and bioterrorism to mention a few. These developments necessarily influence service provision, health spending, including ICT investments, and even health financing. With regard financing, for example, the UK took some controversial measures that may elicit a similar reaction in Canada. Concerned about the likely future burden of healthcare, pensions and social services costs on a dwindling workforce, due to population ageing, the government requested individuals with over a certain amount of savings to pay their nursing or residential home costs, and it matters little if they have to put their homes on the market in order to do so. Let us hope that the situation does not escalate to this extent in Canada although there have been reports over the years of conversion of a notable percentage of defined benefit pension plans to a defined contribution basis. Some private healthcare plans have also followed suit, the idea of limiting financial commitment or liability essentially shifting the healthcare plan's eventual future financial liability to the member rather than sponsor, which in fact it saves future costs increases. While the country's demographics differ little if at all from the UK's, Canada has much fewer people, and this coupled with rigorous strategic initiatives could steer policies in a different direction than in the U.K. New Zealand has undertaken similar far-reaching health reforms, as did the U.K, although both countries have been careful with tapping non-tax revenue sources for health financing, something Canada so far also abhors. The recent brouhaha as the UK Press made it out to be between the British Prime Minister and his Chancellor of the Exchequer over the report of the Turner Commission on Pensions, underscores the continuing search for solutions to financing the country's social and healthcare problems. Lord Turner in his report, due to be published on November 30, 2005, but already leaked to the Press, had recommended increasing the retirement age from 65 years to 67 years as part of pension reforms but the Chancellor opposed this because he believed it flawed and unaffordable. Indeed, the Chancellor, Mr. Gordon Brown, allegedly wrote a letter to Lord Turner, noting the prospects of Government cutting the real value of the pension credit, its key policy for helping poorer pensioners, in as short a period as three years from now. By linking pension credit increase with that of earnings rather than as Brown proposes, that of price index, experts believe the Chancellor s fears about where money to fund state pension would come from are real. Canada spent 10.1% of its Gross Domestic Product (GDP) on health in 2004, and a commitment of $41.3 billion to health over the next and projections suggest that this percentage will likely continue to rise. However, there is no doubt that government is keen to contain health spending, which again makes ongoing reforms imperative, more so in light of the chances of the country eventually having a parallel private health system, which some argue will likely add to the spiraling healthcare costs that governments already bear.

Australia, runs a parallel private health system, hence Canada could learn something from the country's experiences. One key experience being that the country saved little by way of health costs, which is hardly surprising considering the divergent priorities of each health system previously mentioned. On the contrary, government may need to purchase certain services from the private sector, as is the case even now in some provinces. However, by adopting the principles of transaction costs, governments could save substantially, as also previously noted. Australia also did not notice significant reductions in its waiting lists with a parallel private health system operational. Here again, Canada's expectations must be measured because not everyone would be able to afford the services provided outside the public health system and such persons may not have appropriate insurance cover to cover them. Indeed, this underscores the need for governments to continue their respective programs to reduce wait lists in their jurisdictions, many such plans currently in place, largely backed by extensive management information systems and other ICT. The Australian experience also confirms the complexity of the issues involved with the origins and effective management of hospital weight lists, which are unlikely to be identical in different countries. Furthermore, it also suggests the likely need of governments purchasing services from the private health sector as part of its strategy to reduce wait lists. For example would it not be necessary to purchase such services in a city where the only other orthopedic surgeon for example works in the private health system, yet hundreds of senior citizens are waiting in the public health system for years to see the only orthopedic surgeon who evidently is already overwhelmed with work?

It is clear from the foregoing that government may need to purchase services from a parallel health system, and that it needs to develop clear and appropriate policies and mechanisms for so doing, and well in advance, in case this parallel system comes into being nationwide sometime in future. It is also clear that many of the contentious issues in the private versus public health system debate may not be that significant after all considering the complex, and undoubtedly necessary interactions that will ensue in the event of both systems operating in tandem. Indeed, the private health sector will also need the public health system, for example, in integrating their clinical management information systems with government's much broader information databases, which in fact, they may have no option but to do. This may be due to government laws aimed at facilitating disease surveillance in the country, for example, not to mention enhancing real-time information sharing, hence quality of care. The role that ICT will likely play in the effective functioning of either system, and in the collaboration that will occur between them, is immense, as are the challenges in the way. It is therefore important for government to start early looking at permutations of these inevitable interactions at the information and knowledge flow levels, and the various issues involved, for example and crucially, national security, with private health organizations possibly gaining access to vital information that could compromise the country's security. Both parties indeed, need to be concerned about information security, in both with wired and wireless milieus, as they will have to contend with the ceaseless efforts of malicious persons and organizations attempting to access vital patient health and other information for their nefarious purposes. Other issues such as standards and interoperability will become more complex as private health organizations purchase software and ICT from disparate sources, which will compound governments ongoing efforts to address such problems even within it own ranks. Meanwhile private healthcare providers will be facing their own additional problems, such as whether to hook their Microsoft Outlook E-mail clients to Oracle s applications server and store their email messages in its new Oracle 9i database, with a built-in E-mail server, or in Microsoft Exchange, or to invest in the self-defending network technology Cisco recently developed. In short, rather than seriously threaten Medicare, the presence of a parallel private health system, some would argue, creates an interdependence that both systems will have to nurture for their mutual benefit, if not even survival, in the long term, ICT a foremost player in the ensuing dynamics.

Prospects and challenges of private health systems

T he debate over Canada should have a parallel private health system rages on. There are many who are in no doubt that it is just a matter of time before the rest of the country joins Quebec in lifting any legal restraint on an individual seeking private healthcare for whatever reason anywhere in Canada. There must also be many both within and outside the healthcare field already busy at the drawing table ironing out business strategies and plans to venture into the private healthcare business in Quebec and elsewhere in Canada. As with any business enterprise, it would be impetuous for anyone to expect that running a private healthcare operation is going to be all smooth sailing. On the contrary, it is prudent to anticipate hurdles in the way, while keeping the hope of success that presumably inspired the venture alive. What then are the prospects and challenges of private health systems? What role might healthcare ICT play in enhancing these prospects and overcoming the challenges? The Canadian federal government plans to spend C$41 billion over the next decade to improve the public health system burdened by, among other problems, long wait lists, a dearth of healthcare professionals, and of cutting-edge technologies, and bureaucratic deadlocks-the very issues some contend a private health system would be all too ready to exploit for its own gains. The question remains though whether they create true prospects considering the significant funds the federal government plans to inject into the public health system in the next ten years. Would this investment not yield dividends as expected regarding improved healthcare delivery? Would the government's ongoing Health reforms many of which incorporate the "New Public Management" (NPM) paradigm and other principles aimed at modernizing health management in a business-like direction not help loosen bureaucratic deadlocks and improve governance? How could these developments affect the chances of private healthcare providers being profitable? What effect might these developments have on competitiveness in healthcare delivery?

There are several reasons why Canadians presently purchase supplementary insurance, one major reason being the limited coverage for out-of-country healthcare services or none at all. In some provinces, there is even a time limit, 12 months in Ontario for example, for persons who are submitting claims for health services received outside the province or territory or out-of-country. Considering the amount of traveling Canadians do, both within and outside the country, and the fact that one could fall ill or have an accident during any of these trips, it is no doubt important to ensure that one has adequate health insurance coverage. This one area will likely create enormous business opportunities for the private health system. Indeed, healthcare brokerage firms are already springing up in the country, arranging healthcare services and hooking Canadians up with orthopedic surgeons, cardiologists, obstetricians, pediatricians and any other specialist or specific laboratory or diagnostic services they need in the country and abroad. Venture capitalists are also starting to establish healthcare organizations equipped with state-of-the-art technologies and staffed by high-caliber experts, providing services for anyone who could afford them. There will of course be some healthcare professionals, some currently in family practice, others employed by government, who will opt for the private health system, either in solo, or in group practices of various sizes, taking some of their patients along. Allied healthcare professionals such as optometrists, physiotherapists, psychologists, and lab technologists will also feature in the mix, some merging for competitive edge, some affiliating with private hospitals and other healthcare organizations, others actually assimilated via employment or takeovers by bigger industry players. There is likely to be a proliferation of private health clubs and wellness organizations offering sophisticated healthy living and physical exercise programs. Alternative healthcare will likely thrive on its own, or what some refer to as integrated health care, although this is not certain, if other provinces and territories decided to regulate it as British Columbia has done, and as the bill introduced only a few days ago in the Ontario legislature aims to achieve. The interesting point about all these developments is that they will not necessarily involve only persons or organizations with a background in the health industry, but any interested entrepreneur with the financial resources and business acumen. This scenario is precisely the federal government's concern that allowing private health clinics to operate, as is the case in some provinces even now, will ultimately result in a full-fledged second-tier health system albeit by default, and although acknowledging at the same time that it is within the purview of provincial governments to prevent this from happening. Additionally, it is the failure to reach an agreement on the request of the New Democratic Party (NDP) for federal government measures to prevent the scenario that some claim led to the party withdrawing its support for the ruling Liberal Party, which essentially has triggered an election likely in January 2006. In a recent statement in Vancouver, the NDP leader, Mr. Jack Layton, restated the party's position on the issue of private clinics, insisting that the party does not oppose them so long as they do not receive public funds, reminding his audience that private clinics have existed in Canada since the establishment of Medicare[17].

Indeed, in support of Mr. Layton's stand, some would ask whether it is possible to have a competitive free healthcare market, which some claim is what Canada needs, if funded with people's taxes. According to some estimates, as many as thirty private diagnostic clinics currently operate in B.C., Alberta, Quebec, and Nova Scotia, most reimbursed for some of the services they provide with public funds[17]. The federal government on the other hand makes no issue of the existence of autonomous versus partial private clinics, insisting that Ottawa has penalized provinces for violating the Canada Health Act in the past and will continue to do so. Some contend however that it would be difficult to curtail the proliferation of private clinics, and the consequent evolution of a second-tier health system, endorsing Senator Kirby's proposals for privately delivered health care so long as Canadians do not fund it out of pocket. The position Canadian provinces and territories adopt on this issue will determine the nature of the opportunities available to and the intensity of many of the challenges private clinics and healthcare providers will face in the near future, but so will that of the federal government particularly with regard amending and or enforcing the Canada Health Act.

Let us for now assume that the trend continues and more private health clinics emerge, and that they do not receive reimbursements for services covered by Medicare, or any public funding in any guise. Let us also assume that indeed legal rulings eventually legitimize a parallel private health system in other provinces besides, Quebec, perhaps even in the entire country, these private health establishments will find themselves subjected to the full might of market forces. They will also be subject to a variety of government regulations that may more or less restrict their operations and pose significant challenges to their very survival, let alone profitability. Let us start with market forces. It is simple and undeniable that the success of any good or service depends on its value-added propensity to the customer, assuming that it is one the customer wants and will purchase. There is no doubt that people need health services. However, in Canada, they have Medicare, which is free. Any private health service has therefore to offer services Medicare does not offer or cover, or is too slow to provide, for it to make sense for anyone to seek them elsewhere. Furthermore, the private health clinic or healthcare provider has to offer the services at prices the individuals seeking them can afford, or another clinic will not provide cheaper. Indeed, some of the market forces with which these private health establishments would have to contend would be far more complex. There would of course be individuals and circumstances that would flaw the seamless operations of these forces. Some Canadians have sufficient financial resources for example not to care going to British Columbia for a surgical procedure cheaper than in Manitoba where he or she resides, and so might not even some not-so-rich Canadians for a variety of reasons. There may be too little time to shop for services considering the acuteness of an illness or the urgency of the need for care. Government reforms, polices, and regulations may inadvertently skew market forces. Nonetheless, and despite these possible imperfections, private health services are likely to struggle with a variety of market forces that may make or break them in the end.

Some believe that there is a state of hyper-competition in contemporary business community, predicated on the continuing viability of any business on being able to acquire the resources to create strategic alliances, sometimes the means regardless, necessary for innovative businesses to evolve, the ability to outsmart competition in this regard, perhaps the surest path to long-lasting competitive edge. This will likely place many private healthcare providers under pressure not just to stay ahead in the provision of value-added services, but also in developing new marketable products and services, in other words, innovating. Private health clinics must be ready to compete at different levels, first with individual private health clinics, but also with those delivering similar services, with competition stiffest in the latter case, for example, between cardiologists, or orthodontists, rather simply among physicians or dentists. This may mean investing in new ICT, or developing some other innovative and critical elements of value-added client services, or at the very least tracking competition and being able to respond promptly and robustly as warranted, all ingredients of success in a huge industry with varied and bountiful business opportunities. Let us consider the fitness/wellness sector for example. At first, this sector may comprise simply a hodgepodge of gyms, spas, health education classes, and dietary focus groups, but over time, the sector may undergo organic transformation, with more organized business enterprises comprising one or two, even more of these hitherto autonomous disparate groups emerging, some even specializing, in women, the elderly, or in weight control, for examples. This may result in some of the earlier groups withering away, their moribund fates sealed by the more organized and larger entities that have emerged. One may actually start to see a widening of the client base by cross-platform coalescence, essentially, some cardiology group practices teaming up with fitness/wellness enterprises, enriching their value propositions and creative offerings, harnessing more-eclectic financial, human, supply chain, customer service, and other resource pools. Some would argue that this would not only create convenient and client-focused, enhanced and integrated services, but also energize the country's economic base and provide employment opportunities for many. Additionally, that competition would drive down the costs to Canadians of accessing these services, relieving government of heavy involvement in health service provision, hence health spending, which would free-up resources for other public services, and redirect government efforts to policy formulation.

Competition among private healthcare providers will determine the extent to which any particular provider will benefit from the business opportunities its niche offers, and the ability to create value will determine the outcome of this competition and eventually profitability. It is imperative for success that these private health organizations formulate appropriate business strategies for them to stand any chance of surviving in what will likely be an intensely competitive milieu, made even more so by the activities of brokerage firms that will likely become a potent force in patients' choice of physicians and healthcare service providers. The activities of these brokers may not have too great an impact on the patronage of large physician groups with plenty advertisement dollars, but are likely to adversely affect smaller healthcare firms that lack advertisement or public relations leverage. Even with practices that depend on local clientele, they may have much campaigning to do, particularly if they are competing with larger physician groups. These factors will likely be sufficient to keep some doctors away from venturing into the private health system, and others coming right back. For those able to withstand competitive forces, being to do so, in the long term will depend on the interplay of a variety of factors, but underpinning each organization's performance will be its leadership. No organization will succeed steered by a leadership bankrupt in ideas and entombed in outlook. The role of the leader is so crucial some, for example, Maccoby[18], in his book, The Productive Narcissist: The Promise and Peril of Visionary Leadership, do not hesitate to argue that a productive narcissist may even be the best leader an organization needs in an era of disruptive changes such as ours. He described the need in leadership for foresight, systems thinking, visioning, motivating, and partnering, attributes he referred to collectively as "strategic intelligence". How would a leader, who for one reason or another is unable to see the need to have an ICT strategy for example, appreciate the defining role technology plays in differentiating and in enhancing competition? Is the healthcare organization that has such a leader not doomed from the start? What about a leader who takes cost-based strategizing to an extreme and fails to recognize that not all investments in healthcare service provision yields immediate returns on investment (ROI), or one that is unable to touch the creative nerve of employees and motivate them to develop innovative ideas that will add value to the organization's service mix? How is an organization likely to fare under such defective leadership? Herein then is another major challenge some private healthcare providers will face and one that may compromise their organization to possibly the point of extinction. The lure of independence and a ready, wide-open market will likely be quite strong, and in the beginning, attract some healthcare professionals into the private health system. Many of them may not however, realize how ill equipped they are to run a business, which is essentially what they will be doing, except perhaps, they have the resources to employ a full-time manager, even when it would be tactless not to keep an eye on how the manager is running their business.

One of the first things that a doctor or any other healthcare professional aspiring to establish a private practice, in the event of a parallel private health system emerging in Canada needs to do is a self-reorientation toward a business mindset. Healthcare professionals will need to appreciate how competitive forces could ruin them in no time and learn all they could about how the business world works. Indeed, such physicians and other healthcare professionals will have to communicate their vision and mission of the practices they set up to their managers and other employees, and should not have managers that are unable to complete a migration path audit successfully, or align operating initiatives with strategic vision, for example. Of course, some doctors would prefer to seek employment in a for-profit private hospital or some such organization founded by medical or even non-medical entrepreneurs and venture capitalists, or even insurance companies, or anyone with the money to do so, for that matter. Healthcare professionals who find themselves in this situation will need major adjustments to make or will soon find themselves out of jobs. For-profit healthcare organizations are even more likely to operate under strict business rules and have little patience or tolerance for any actions or attitudes that its management or board considers inimical to corporate interests. There are several reasons why the "owners" of private, for-profit health institutions may become impatient with doctors and other healthcare professionals who are slow to adapt to the "rules" of business operations. Consider the following scenarios. Assume for example that there is no real competition between the public an private health systems, for example, because the public system still underwrites certain services that they provide when obtained in the private system, or sell quotas for surgical operations to the private health system for, say, the lack of relevant professionals, or to reduce wait lists. Under these circumstances, private health organizations are making money from public funds and the private patients that pay on their own or via employer insurance schemes. A surgeon, for example employed by such for-profit organizations, which as it is with them to seek profits while minimizing costs, may find the workload or working hours increasing without a commensurate increase in remuneration if it did at all. Another private health organization struggling to acquire clientele and keep them may attempt to extract more from the surgeon, again, without necessarily offering more pay. In both instances, the employer may not hesitate to fire any uncooperative surgeon or employee for that matter. For-profit organizations are also unlikely to tolerate anyone that seems too slow in adapting to the often-frenetic pace of the business world, for example, in learning to use some new technology, or showing a lack of interest in doing so. However, healthcare organizations intent on driving the for-profit principles to extremes may find themselves confronting the organized union activities of certain healthcare professional groups, sometimes with unsavory consequences for the organizations bottom line, even image in healthcare markets. Doctors are used to being the team leaders in patient management. Those doctors that opt for the private sector will likely discover a totally different hierarchical arrangement, with the decision-making about patient management influenced by factors and individuals outside their control, for examples, strict policies regarding the use of equipments, medication prescriptions, lab investigations, even ICT, often with an underlying profit motive. Such a situation may create ethical conflicts for the healthcare professional that may be serious enough to warrant considering resignation. Challenges may also surface with new government regulations regarding medical licensure and practice, as may many others the doctor or other healthcare professional contemplating leaving the public for the private health system in case the latter evolves in the country may not anticipate, or can handle. The point then is that the private sector is different form the public sector in many ways. It is in general a tougher and less secure work environment than the public sector. True, many of the private health institutions will attempt to attract doctors and other healthcare professionals into their institutions, but with the prospects of more earnings may come some horrid experiences.

Besides the individual challenges that physicians will likely face, the organizations they work with will have challenges of their own, and good leadership is not the only of, or the panacea to these challenges, which may be local, regional, provincial, national, or global. The customer base of a private health system may include individuals, health insurers, and governments, other private health organizations for example nursing homes, and private firms that may retain their services. These clients would likely seek the best services, and would readily change their healthcare providers in order to receive the needed services if necessary. Private healthcare providers are well aware of this and are likely to remain in business because they do whatever necessary to prevent it. With regard to individuals, the services private clinics provide must be of such higher standards than in government hospitals for anyone to want to pay for them rather than obtain them free, except if the trouble of queuing on a long wait list outweighs the benefits of the latter choice. Indeed, government, for policy determination, and private health institutions, for competitive strategizing, may indeed be keen to determine whether private health systems outperform public health systems. They could perform this exercise by evaluating if the emergence of private health system increased the quality adjusted life years (QALY)/ per unit cost, for example. They could also do so by finding out how the unit cost per quality adjusted life years (QALY) the former generates fare with the latter. These exercises would require cost utility analysis for example determining the unit cost of an average case mix standardized unit of medical or surgical treatment in both settings, or the comparing the rates and costs of the Quality adjusted life years (QALY) both settings generated in a specific period. The results of these calculations may mean little to the average individual seeking healthcare services, but may significantly influence their choice of service providers, albeit on the advice of health services brokers, some of whom may be calculating and examining such figures. Health insurers are also likely to be interested in statistics and outcome data not just for actuarial reasons but to choose the most cost-effective healthcare providers for their clients, the right to make those determinations likely incorporated into certain categories of insurance covers. Furthermore, why should government not trumpet its achievements if its figures were better than those of the private health system were and why would clients be streaming to the latter under those circumstances? Patients are therefore not simply going to be out there for the taking by private healthcare providers. On the contrary, these providers will have to work hard to obtain and retain them. They will also have to contend with government regulations that will likely be in place to protect individuals from any sort of exploitation by the private healthcare providers on the one hand, and private health insurers and brokers on the other. Even legislation binding on the latter two, for example on the privacy and security of patient information, or ICT governance, could have indirect, even direct consequences on the operations of private healthcare providers.

Supplemental insurance has been part of the Canadian health system all along. Such insurance coverage people buy or their employers purchase for them for services Medicare does not cover, and these services vary from province to province. Some would argue that governments in Canada are reducing covered expenses and de-insuring some basic healthcare coverage and that individuals, private health insurers, employers, and workers' associations are the ones picking up bills. Some contend this is to reduce wait lists, others that it is money saving. Canada businesses spend $33 billion in mental illness disability costs annually, some of the costs likely due in part to morbidity, sometimes prolonged, and some argue, patients' inability to afford medications not covered by Medicare once out of hospital in some provinces engender. However, governments at F/ P/ T levels seem to be taking notice and action, and reasonably so, no government would want to see the recent General Motors debacle, which has led to the loss of thousands of jobs in the company, and now Ford Motors, with a likely similar end-result, reenacted in Canada.. The Alberta government, for example, is investing $75 million into new mental health projects in the province approved under the Mental Health Innovation Fund, and part of new three-year health plans developed by the province's nine regional health authorities (RHA), to provide a variety of mental health services. The projects are specific to each region's needs and within the framework of the overall mental health services goals of the province, within an even more inclusive, some would say controversial, Third Way Plan for healthcare[19]. Nary an instance would one likely find of a province without restrictions on its basic healthcare coverage. However, Medicare has never covered every aspect of healthcare and probably would it ever, not with the seeming exponential increases in health spending with no end in sight. Projections of Canada's healthcare spending in 2001 exceed C$100 billion. Canada plans to infuse approximately $41 billion into its health system over a decade, and its 2005 health budget will add $2.5 billion to Canada Health Transfer, increasing the base to $19 billion, which itself will increase yearly by six percent, in keeping with the 'escalator clause.' The country spent $15 billion on prescription and non-prescription drugs in 2001, $12.3% on just the former 10.6% more than it did in 2000. Its drug expenditures for 2004 were $21.4 billion in 2004, 8.8 percent more than the previous year, and five times more than it spent in 1985, prescription drugs walloping $18-billion, up 10.2 per cent from 2003. With its average annual real per capita growth for hospitals/ physicians, and prescribed drugs, being, 3% and 10% respectively, according to figures the Canadian Institute for Health Information released in May 2005[20], some wonder if government simply could afford to keep spending such huge proportions of its budget on health. Others, if it were not in fact justified shedding some of Medicare coverage and seeking ways to contain health spending. Yet others caution that while fiscal prudence makes sense, the issues need looked at in relevant perspectives. For example, only Nova Scotia, Ontario, and Quebec, had growth rates below the national average for total P/ T government health expenditures, and for specific expenditures, British Columbia had expenditure growth over the national average for hospitals, other institutions (primarily residential care facilities for seniors), and physicians, and below national average for other professionals and prescribed drugs. The Northwest Territories had reversed growth rates for similar categories. On the surface, these figures suggest that some provinces are spending even more on health, or some aspect of it, than the national average, but do they suggest that the health status of those not spending as much is inferior, or that private insurers should be flocking to those places because governments there are spending less on health? The expenditure per capita, and indeed, the health status of the jurisdiction spending less may just be above the national average. On the other hand, the province or territory that is seemingly spending more may be making up for lost time or paying more for same service usage levels with its citizens health status not necessarily having improved. Health insurers or private health clinics or organizations hoping to base business judgments on these figures will need cost-benefit or cost-effectiveness analysis for any such judgment to be meaningful. Furthermore how would the fact that aging-specific effect will have only minimal contribution annually to P/ T government total health expenditures between 2002 and 2026, although more, 2.6%, on other institutions category influence evaluation of business opportunities by private health insurers and healthcare providers? Does this point to the significant chunk of health spending younger people consume? Would this change the 12% to 18% overall annual inflation factors private health insurers apply to survive increasing costs, or the terms of health care plans? Does any private health insurer or healthcare provider need to know that expenditures per capita for both sexes are under C$1000 until after the age group, 45 to 65 years, when they start to rise sharply, becoming higher for males than females in all senior age groups? Should this be surprising considering morbidity is higher for males than it is for females with cardiovascular disease, the leading cause of mortality and hospital costs in the country? Mortality rate for all cardiovascular diseases for both sexes in Canada was 200.9 per 100,000 Population in 2001, next most prevalent cause of deaths being cancer (all types) with a mortality rate of 179.1 per 100,000 population, with estimated hospital costs for the former in 1998 being about $4.2 billions, followed by mental disorders, with about $2.7 billions. Are these figures and other important health statistics likely to change, why, and in which direction, and should private healthcare providers also be paying attention, as government must be?

A major challenge private healthcare providers will face is not only being familiar with health indicators, at least in their operational areas, but also collecting health data, and transforming them into valuable information, and finally actionable knowledge. This will not only require investments in relevant ICT, but may warrant the services of knowledge managers particularly by the larger establishments and those able to afford such services. An exercise such as that would be invaluable for strategic service planning, and better prospects of return on investments and profitability. Not long ago, the Alberta Insurance Act changed, requiring disability plans covering its residents insured if they provided benefits of over two years' duration. Although there were a few exceptions to this new law, the challenge it posed for many self-insured disability plan sponsors, particularly national plans with few Albertans was indisputable. How could such legislative changes influence the ideas of health plan sponsors and employers of say, group benefit plans being a notable aspect of compensation packages and could such laws make them more proactive in managing their benefit programs? How could this attitudinal change influence sponsor/ private health insurer/ healthcare provider relationships? What effects might the new dispensation, for example, plans sponsors educating their members, which ICT could aid and make more effective, about provider choices based on costs and service quality, or limiting reimbursement to current drug formularies, or cost sharing, for examples, have on cost containment and in effect on business opportunities for private health insurers and providers? What effects could aggressive cost control by plans sponsors such as prescription drug dispensing fee caps, have on the private health industry? In addition to the challenges, private firms and other plans sponsors that retain their services pose to private healthcare providers, nursing homes, and government hospitals may have direct business dealings with private healthcare providers that may provide opportunities but also may create tension between the partners, either in terms of disputes over costs, or services provided, or lack thereof. Private healthcare providers will also have to sustain the quality of service provision, at the very least, if not actually have to improve it, to retain these clients, particular if they previously had some sort of monopoly in a given jurisdiction that they no longer have. Perhaps the more challenging aspect of the relationship between private healthcare providers and government will be regarding legislative and regulatory control over aspects of their operations, many with direct consequences on their bottom line. Here though, one might hear the cautions of those wary of the damaging effects of over-regulation on the overall economy of the country, particularly in an increasingly globalized market.

By far the toughest challenge that will confront the private health system is surviving in a highly competitive market. To start with, it is becoming more difficult for healthcare organizations to raise money. This is ironic happening when they need money the most for capital projects, to develop clinical programs, employ professionals, and invest in ICT, among others, ICT alone usually constituting up to 30% of the capital budget of a healthcare system. Since many, if not all private healthcare system will need to seek funds, even operating funds, at some point they will have to start making the necessary adjustments to enable them raise these funds. These adjustments include defining and focusing on their business strategy, embracing financial discipline, improving their bottom line, and being ready to convince their proposed creditors of the sense in their planned capital projects, among others. In particular, with ICT investments taking up such a significant proportion of the capital budget, CEOs of healthcare organizations have a crucial challenge of explaining how ICT supports the establishment s business objectives, whether it facilitates or competes with clinical program development, if it yields returns on investments (ROI), and what measures are in place to manage it cost-effectively. With competition for clients in the health industry largely shaped by the ability of a healthcare provider to meet the needs of an increasingly demanding and sophisticated clientele, and with ICT a major player in acquiring and retaining clientele, there is no gainsaying the enormity of this challenge and the importance of overcoming it. Considering that, there is evidence that healthcare providers that utilize ICT tend to perform better solving critical business problems[23], not to mention the cost-saving benefits of ICT and those of improving the quality of healthcare delivery, perhaps would justify the efforts. Healthcare organizations should also optimize their legacy systems, integrating them into workflows and processes, enhancing and reusing software to make them last longer, rather than embarking on their wholesale replacement at the slightest excuse. ICT investments should aim at solving business or clinical problems. The goal should be streamlining work processes, or facilitating information sharing, for examples, rather wanting to purchase a scheduling system or just any solution for that matter. Management should be keener to identify opportunities to enhance current and create new services that will increase the value offering and set the organization apart from its competitors, hence attract more clients, and increase its revenue and profitability, that incorporating appropriate ICT strategic initiatives in the organizations overall long term goals offer. By so doing, it would be much easier for management to demonstrate the tangible and intangible value of ICT, its risks, and costs, and its chances of yielding ROI, making it even easier to raise the funds required to actualize the proposed project.

Being able to raise funds is one thing, utilizing the funds in ways that would not only yield ROI but that would enhance the healthcare organization's competitiveness is another, perhaps even more important in the long term, and that is the key challenge many private healthcare providers would have to confront. There is hardly any doubt that regarding the need for a clear and compelling strategic orientation for any healthcare organization, its size regardless, to survive in today's hypercompetitive business milieu. Additionally, strategy has to be distinct, reflecting the organization's business objectives and vision, and officialdom, inertia, and pettiness, should not bog down its execution. It may sound absurd, but even visions and long-term goals may become archaic, if based on faulty premises and inadequate information and knowledge, for example, of the direction of technological progress or the evolution of medical knowledge. The organization's strategy must create value, and in abundance, as only this could result in client satisfaction, sustained growth and revenues, investor confidence, and shareholder returns. The organization wants to be unique and to create new markets, breaking through from the crowd, and becoming a market leader, all of which are possible via strategic intent rooted in a thorough understanding and continuing appraisal of the multiplicity of forces impinging on the business, and of the best ways to navigate the path in the industry to success. ICT could help in achieving these objectives for example provided the organization does not let it become pretty much a commodity, but a veritable value-creation resource aligned strategically to the organizations vision and business goals. Healthcare ICT helps contain costs, free and optimize resources, and enhance competitiveness. It increases productivity, an improves quality of care delivery in a number of ways including making critical patient information available at the point of care (POC), and reducing medical error rates. Appropriate use of the Internet, for example, promotes patient-focused care, empowering patients to participate actively in their healthcare, thereby creating an enabling environment to transform healthcare delivery for the better. This is addition to the role of ICT in improving the non-medical processes of the organization, for examples, its administrative and financial management processes. The organization s strategy must be multi-platform. There is a tendency for many organizations to focus overly on costs savings. To be sure, there is nothing wrong with budgetary control to preserve scarce resources for future utilization, but this should be only one of the strategy platforms that any organization should embrace. An organization should also have, for examples, policy-based strategies that develop effective policies for building sustainable competitiveness; structure-based strategies aimed at establishing a firm, efficient, and mission-driven platform for transactions and other business operations; and ICT, product/ services development, and sales/ marketing strategies, among others. These and other business-related concepts some healthcare professionals do not employ in their routine activities but are concepts that they need to be familiar with and ready to imbibe and utilize if planning to operate independently in a private heath system.

Healthcare providers new to management principles and practices and those familiar with them need to be aware of the danger of becoming lost in a maze of management theories. The field is in such flux that some of these theories have an incredibly short life span, which is healthy for the field as none whose knowledge base remains static will not in time is a dodo. Nonetheless, the last thing any new entrant into the business world needs is a cacophony of ideas on every conceivable management task. Suffice to know that there is going to be competition out there and it could be quite stiff, and that the new healthcare organization needs to have a strong grasp of basic management principles. These include mapping out its strategy to confront the challenges competition brings well in advance, ascertaining the flawless execution of these strategies, simplifying organizational structure for effective and speedy realization of objectives, and nurturing a culture of creativity, excellence, and commitment to the ideals of the organization, part of which incidentally requires appropriate remuneration for performance. The healthcare organization needs to decide early what its core services are, say to provide medical services at affordable prices to children and adolescents, and stick with them, developing services and products to meet their changing needs, keeping its focus on its strategy laser sharp, and not foraying outside its strategic market niche in a latently suicidal flip-flop. It should also not be selling hair care products, for example, in an in-house store carved out of its business premises, or operating a while-u-wait pizza service, a move that would fudge its focus and confuse its clients. On the other hand, it may need to locate its clinics in low-income areas or in high-browse suburban parts of town depending on its preferred targets as stated in its clear and doable strategic goals. The idea is for the healthcare provider, as a starting point, to develop a clear strategy and communicate it from time to time to the target clientele, employees, and shareholders, in an equally clear and focused value proposition based on just as lucid and honest appraisal of the organization's core competencies and knowledge of its target clients and markets. The other side of this is that the organization should be cautious about pursuing growth, which sometimes drives unwary executives into taking their firms into alien domains, often with disastrous consequences. This suggests that growth, including via acquisitions and mergers, is an option, leaving room to tweak strategy in response to changes in government regulations, health trends and indicators, or scientific knowledge and technological progress, for examples. It is doubtful that doctors will be able or keen to add much more business information to their already-overloaded information store than is basic. They may therefore need the services of professional managers to handle the business side of their practice, although this may be difficult or unrealistic in solo practices, mostly because of the cost implications, in which case, such doctors would need more than rudimentary business knowledge for the practice to survive. They would also need to know about management practice tools, and how to use them for example to facilitate execution such as Kaizen, Total Quality Management (TQM), or Six Sigma, the latter a process sometimes termed a measure of quality that strives for near perfection. It will likely sufficiently satisfy most clients that their healthcare providers met their expectations, and would probably care less that they exceeded them. Nonetheless, it is ideal to strive for perfection, particularly if it is part of the value proposition, provided it is realistic, for example setting goals for service quality improvement in specific areas that create the most value for clients, rather than attempting to do so in many areas at once. Besides wasting scarce resources, the organization may not achieve the stated objectives in any of the areas, or the expected increased patient turnover. It is also important for quality improvement and the smooth running of the organization not to swamp it with policies, regulations, or bureaucracy, and in the interests of not just the employees, but also the clients, and the organization too. Indeed, by making the organization flatter, middle management is able to take important decisions without struggling along a long command chain, fostering creativity, ownership of projects, ethical responsibility, and commitment to the organization's ideals and objectives, even attracting new and enthusiastic personnel.

There is no doubt about the immensity of the challenges healthcare providers would face in the event of a parallel private health system emerging in Canada, and that an article such as this is unlikely to cover them all. It is not certain that a parallel private health system will emerge in Canada, although some believe that the recent Supreme Court decision declaring Quebec's ban on private healthcare for services Medicare covers invalid, signals the onset of the eventual emergence of a parallel private health system in the entire country. In this regard, and considering the presence in the country even now of a certain degree of private health care, it is likely that some physicians, and even non-medical entrepreneurs and venture capitalists are already contemplating establishing private healthcare businesses and facilities in the country. Considering also, the importance of health to survival, and some of the problems the current public health system struggle with, there is little doubt that there are prospects for market penetration by these budding private healthcare providers. The challenges are however substantial, as the foregoing clearly shows. How many of the new, and even existing private healthcare providers that will survive these challenges, particularly in the long term, remains speculative. This is more so that government will likely not be sitting idly by watching the operations of a market that, just as any, is likely inherently flawed. How much would the federal government interfere under those circumstances? What would be the nature of such regulation? Would the regulations buoy government's own efforts to improve healthcare delivery in the public health system, stipulating compliance with stiff standards for the private health system? An example of the latter scenario would be government requesting every private healthcare provider to implement healthcare ICT for example electronic medical records systems (EMR) to enable communication with its electronic health records (EHR) project, or to ensure reporting of adverse drug events (ADE), or to facilitate disease surveillance. These measures could qualify as aimed at improving quality of patient care, or facilitating government health programs, both with which nothing there is nothing wrong, but maybe not for cash-strapped private healthcare professionals feeling pressured when perhaps unprepared for those sorts of expenditures.

Government is always looking for ways to deliver health services to Canadians in accordance with the Canada Health Act, and will likely continue to do so despite the emergence of a private health system in the country. It will also likely be seeking ways to reduce health spending over time without compromising health services delivery. It will be looking for novel ways to promote health, to prevent and mange diseases, and to deliver health services efficiently, and cost-effectively. It will likely be doing so acknowledging the imperatives of competition, the need to deliver increasing value to clients. This will necessitate appropriate public services reform, including instituting more New Public management (NPM) principles that will streamline operations and enhance productivity, in turn facilitating the delivery of high quality services. This will likely obviate the need for many Canadians to resort to private health services except it becomes unavoidable, a potential serious challenge to the viability of private healthcare services now or down the road. Some would argue that such issues question the need for the private v. public health system debate in the first place since a precarious symbiosis may emerge from their respective organic evolution that may threaten to keep both systems operating tiptop. Matters would have been different were government intent on privatizing the public health system, although some of the reforms the system would likely undergo some would contend amount to privatizing it, which would not be true in totality, particularly as funding would not be coming from non-tax revenue sources such as user fees, among others. Yet, there would need to be some re-orienting in the public health system to a business-like approach to running healthcare that would make it more cost-effective to run and more competitive in the wake of an emergent private health system. Even with the pursuit of excellence in the public health system having an egalitarian motive, any private healthcare would still have to work quite hard to attract clients from and compete successfully with it. This is the reality of free market, but juxtaposed with effective public health services, some may ask if society would not have a healthier and productive citizenry with copious employment opportunities from which to choose, and if this should not erase any angst on both sides of and make the debate on private v. public health system redundant.

The business value of ICT in health systems

Projected health spending in Canada in 2005 is $142 billion, about 10.4% of the country's GDP (10.1% in 2004), the highest ever, according to data the Canadian Institute for Health Information (CIHI) released on December 07, 2005[24]. Overall increase in health spending over 2004, is 7.7%, and adjusted for inflation rate 5.5%. Government's response to this increase, blamed on an 11% hike in spending on prescription and non-prescribed medication, is not apathetic, not least, because the increasing spending on medications is significantly greater than any other health spending, including on hospital services and doctors remuneration, not to mention depleting resources needed to run other public services. On the contrary, F/ P/ T authorities are seeking ways to control and contain these exorbitant healthcare and particularly drugs costs. Michael Decter, Chair of the Health Council of Canada recently noted that a task force is to report to federal, provincial, and territorial health ministers on issues of drug costs and drug plan coverage in June 2006. There are certainly indications for such measures but could healthcare ICT for example, computerized physician order entry (CPOE), help reduce spending on medications, and indeed, could healthcare ICT help contain overall health spending? Could it in fact do even more to improve health systems, in Canada? From 1997 to 2003, the Canadian government invested about $1.5 billion in a number of health-related ICT projects, funded through different federal organizations and entities, including Health Canada, Human Resource Development Canada, Industry Canada, National Defence, Veterans Affairs, and CANARIE Inc. The government spent C$ 126 million in 2004 on Healthcare ICT through Canada Health Infoway, and planned to spend $195 million, 56% more in 2005. Canadian provinces are also investing in healthcare ICT. Alberta, for example, allocated $2.6 million from its Telehealth Clinical Services Grant Fund to twenty-one new telehealth initiatives in 2005. Indeed, the province also has a $66 million Alberta Physician Office System Program, which is in collaboration with the Alberta Medical Association, and under which every doctor in Alberta is eligible to receive $7,700 in each of four years to install, undergo training in, and start using electronic medical records (EMR) in his/ her practice. More than 50% of its doctors have responded. Ontario is investing $57 million over five years to support patient care through ICT, and it plans to invest another $45 million on additional diagnostic equipments, including mobile equipments between 2003 and 2006. Saskatchewan invested $2.527 billion in health care in 2003/ 04, 7.9%, or $184 million more than the year before. In the same period, the province gave Regional Health Authorities, $19 million in capital equipment to purchase CT scanners, surgical, and therapeutic equipment, and British Columbia will likely build on its $10 million investment in 2004/05 alone to enhance patient safety, much of the funds for ICT projects. Indeed, there is hardly any Canadian province, or territory not investing or planning to invest substantially in healthcare ICT. Why is this so, and what benefits do these various governments hope to derive from investing in healthcare ICT? Does ICT have any business value in health systems? If so, is it enduring, and how could health systems, public or private determine, and benefit from this business value?

The 1998 report of the National Roundtable on Health Care Quality of the U.S Institute of Medicine (IOM) noted the country's poor quality of health care [25]. Two other IOM reports, "Crossing the Quality Chasm [26]" and "To Err Is Human[27]" were equally revealing. The former identified the quality gaps in healthcare delivery and called for an urgent fundamental change to close the gap, essentially a redesign of the American health care system. It also offers a set of performance expectations for the 21st century health care system, a set of 10 new rules to guide patient-clinician relationships, and suggested an organizing framework to better align incentives inherent in payment and accountability with quality improvement, as well as major steps to promote evidence-based practice and strengthen clinical information systems. The latter report highlighted the high medical error rates in US hospitals. All three reports acknowledged the important role healthcare ICT could play in improving healthcare delivery. In support of the reports, a number of different healthcare stakeholders, including governments, not-for and for-profit organizations, payers, and the public have been advocating patient safety, confidentiality and security of patient information, healthcare quality, affordability, and have been promoting health ICT adoption, which they believe could help achieve these goals. The Leapfrog Group, a coalition of large and influential buyers of healthcare in the US, in particular, and others are even offering incentives, including recognizing and rewarding health-oriented quality improvement initiatives[28], by healthcare providers, to facilitate healthcare ICT diffusion. Leapfrog has named CPOE as one of the three significant "leaps" healthcare providers need to take to improve patient safety. Indeed, starting in 2006, The Leapfrog Group and Med-Ventage, a San Francisco based consulting and informatics company specializing in pay for performance (P4P) designs, measures, and reporting models, will collaborate on a national survey and compendium tracking all incentive and pay-for-performance programs, whether aimed at health plans, providers, or consumers. This exercise will enable the development of a more comprehensive database for the Leapfrog Incentives and Rewards Compendium, and is part of efforts to encourage healthcare ICT adoption in the health industry. Cost considerations, technophobia, apathy, intimidation by change, and fear of litigation for breach of privacy and confidentiality are some of the reasons the medical community has been lukewarm towards ICT, and which explain why some organizations, such as The Leapfrog Group consider it prudent to offer it incentives. There are also technical difficulties in the way of healthcare ICT diffusion, for example, that posed for interoperability of health information systems by the lack of uniformity of standards, and in some instances of any at all. However, just as important in getting end users to accept and use healthcare ICT is the technologies being available in the first place, and perhaps the most potent hindrance to this being so is what some consider the questionable business value of healthcare ICT investments.

It is not difficult to see why some question the business sense in investing in healthcare ICT, despite its acknowledged benefits in many areas of healthcare delivery. To be sure, this skepticism has not always been this widespread. Indeed, many exalted the economic validity of healthcare ICT investments in those early days, almost four decades ago when financial and administrative applications such as for those billing, and for appointment scheduling, produced measurable and frequently impressive results translatable into visible improvement in productivity, and in returns of investment (ROI). Today, not even the apparently bedazzled hospital chief information officer (CIO) that ballyhoo his or her proposed new cutting-edge clinical information systems could be certain of how to explain to the chief executive officer (CEO), the need to secure funds to procure technologies whose business value is difficult, some would insist, even impossible to determine. Yet, CEOs regularly confront questions regarding investment trade-offs. Unlike financial or administrative information systems, it is more difficult to measure the business value of ICT utilized in patient care, although its benefits to the quality of care delivery leave no one in doubt. It is even more problematic determining the business value in public health systems, where the emphasis is not on revenue generation, but rather on cost control and containment, compared to the private health system, which is keener to see the former outweigh the latter for its healthcare ICT investments to make business sense. Nonetheless, both public and private health systems need to know the business value of whatever their investments may be, since resources are inherently scarce, hence optimization, imperative. The question is how to determine this business value, and it is one that experts have grappled with, and the answers they obtained to which they continue to fine-tune.

Before considering methodological issues, including approaches to determining return on investment (ROI), which may be a convenient, although not necessarily the easiest or best way to measure business value, particularly in the healthcare arena, a brief historical excursion would lay the foundation for a thorough appraisal of the key issues pertaining to the business value of healthcare ICT. As previously mentioned, the days when the business value of implemented information systems in the health sector caused little trouble to assess sharply contrast with the status of ICT in today's healthcare milieu. This is because the relatively easy measurability of ICT business value in the past, stimulated interests in IT investments, whereas the woolliness that envelopes such evaluations these days would in part suggest, and reasonably so, the current seeming apathy towards investing in healthcare ICT. One could also argue that the unfulfilled promises of the early clinical-oriented information systems, despite the substantial amounts of money they gulped, only further convinced the financiers of such projects that investing in healthcare ICT was simply not a smart thing to do. Without attempting to hold brief for software developers and others involved in these projects, the software development process had its woes, some inherent in the intangible nature of the product, others, the difficulties the field encountered dealing effectively with these problems and its ongoing struggles with methodological conundrums. Indeed, some of these difficulties so argue have in the past, led the evolution of ICT along a convoluted, some may even insist, somewhat errant path. How many millions of dollars went into the so-called "solutions" ICT professionals prescribed for businesses and organizations, including healthcare providers in the last two decades or so that failed to deliver on lofty performance promises, for example? Delays in delivering working products, incessant bug fixings, and budget overruns, used to be rampant, but at whose expense were they? Healthcare organizations are unlikely to tolerate these problems these days. They can no longer afford to invest in poorly designed ICT that lack post-implementation support, and is unaligned to organizational, business, and professional needs, as financial resources dwindle with creditors more stringent, yet the demand for health services keep rising and becoming more complex. Healthcare providers will unlikely anymore simply issue a request for proposal (RFP) to purchase, willy-nilly, a new system, because the old one fell out of favor, or an enthusiastic salesperson has been trumpeting the benefits of a new top-of-line replacement "solution." Additionally, there is increasing need for communication and information among different functional units of a hospital, and between hospitals, and with other healthcare agencies, a goal that the deployment of appropriate and reliable ICT would help achieve, improving operations, the quality of healthcare delivery, while also reducing costs. Today's dispensation therefore requires collaboration between healthcare organizations and software vendors, and other ICT professionals in developing healthcare ICT aligned to and aimed at improving the organizations' workflow and other operations, which should enable building a sound business case in order to secure the necessary funds for its implementation.

ICT used to run ledgers or major business information, for example, inventory, or other core applications provided strong support for businesses. In contemporary businesses, including healthcare organizations, ICT plays a more diffuse role, featuring in decision analysis, product and service development, customer service, supply chain management, facilities management, even future studies. ICT has therefore become pervasive, hence its risks ever more intertwined with business risks, creating even more pressure on the CEO to sort out the differences. For example, investments in ICT do not end with its purchase and installation. The CEO also needs to know the likely follow-up financial commitments, for examples, maintenance, software licensing, and with technology changing rapidly and software viruses emerging in numbers, upgrades, and enhancements costs. Furthermore, the CEO also needs to appreciate the business and organizational dynamics of IT, including ensuring IT alignment not just to business goals but also to corporate culture. These issues, and there are many more, particularly in the healthcare industry, highlight the multidimensional nature of the business value of ICT. In the past, software vendors simply developed software and marketers sold them. It was easy to do that then because businesses ran software organized around centralized mainframe computers. Now, businesses need to integrate customer service, sales, inventory, and purchasing information, for examples, and connect this to their suppliers and customers. Software vendors therefore have changed their approach and now collaborate with businesses via their analysts, and other trained professionals, on determining how ICT can meet their client's business needs. Businesses are now keener to deploy ICT in order to streamline and improve the efficiency and effectiveness of their business processes, and to achieve these goals while cutting costs, enhancing the chances of returns on their investments (ROI). In the healthcare industry for example, automating critical organizational processes can significantly improve operations. For example, hospitals consume generous quantities of routine supplies, such as bandages, adhesives, antiseptics, and toiletries. Let us suppose that a hospital purchases these products from a number of different suppliers, keeps them in in-house stockroom inventories, from where it distributes them to where needed, and when, in the hospital. The hospital manager soon figures that there are more efficient and cost-effective ways

52

to manage the hospital's purchases and inventories. He or she then installs computer terminals in the casualty, nursing bays, operating theatres, clinics, and other key locations in the hospital that use the supplies, and links these terminals to the computer of a particular supplier. The terminals record supplies as consumed, and the supplier's computer tracks each location's utilization rates, and then prints a list of needed suppliers at the warehouse, the supplies promptly delivered to the right hospital location. The hospital receives monthly usage statistics from the supplier, clarifying utilization patterns, facilitating resource optimization, and planning and budgeting. The hospital no longer needs to maintain extra inventory, saving money and space, and because the suppliers deliver the items directly to the locations where needed, also reducing labor costs. Furthermore, businesses also want to be able to leverage their IT investments across not just existing but also new markets. They want to be able to determine how technology could help them develop, promote, market, sell, and deliver products and services. Businesses now view ICT as an enabler of business opportunities, and invest in technology to solve business problems, directly or indirectly, and not for its own sake, and the healthcare industry should not be different. ICT could help private healthcare providers create the distinction in service provision crucial to acquiring and sustaining competitive advantage, and the public health system meet its commitment to provide comprehensive and qualitative health services. Yet again, they need to be able to convince their creditors of the need for such investments, that they have business value, including identifying the critical success factors that contribute to this value, and the management's ability to nurture the presumed value into fruition. Private healthcare providers also need to demonstrate the financial returns that would likely accrue from the investments. This is more so as healthcare ICT expenditures have to compete with other important uses of increasingly limited resources, which incidentally is also true for public health systems. Perhaps we ought to note here the importance of intangible benefits, the need to implement IT due to legal or regulatory constraints, with the implications of remaining in business such compliance guarantees. For example, some US states have adopted legislation mandating healthcare providers to publish the pricing of medical procedures for the public to see. This may also happen in Canada when and if a parallel private health system becomes operational in the country, for example. Mistakes seem to occur quite often in charge masters of hospitals and other healthcare providers that seem more concerned about discountable cost-plus markups for managed care rates, than with pricing. There is little doubt that making such errors public knowledge could have adverse image consequences. This is why healthcare organizations need to undertake regular pricing audits. It is in their best interest to compare their pricing to those of their peers that provide similar services, and audit supplies markups and to implement IT capable of ensuring the accuracy of the pricing data and of the data the organization intends to publish. This will not only ensure that they are complying with legal pricing provisions, it will save them unnecessary embarrassment publishing erroneous or unrealistic pricing. Competitive pricing fosters revenue yields. It will likely be ever more important for healthcare providers to price their services correctly and to ensure that they are competitive with the increasing tendency of employers to offer high deductible insurance products and healthcare savings accounts (HSA) as cost-saving benefits options, and with paying patients seeking the best value for their money. This example illustrates the need sometimes to invest in ICT without necessarily expecting a return on that investment, with respect to meeting the requirements of the law for example, although not having the healthcare organization shut down for non-compliance still even indirectly meets a business objective, that of remaining operational. Incidentally, the example, also shows how such investments, which management might essentially have written off in their capital as not going to yield an ROI, doing so not just by enabling the organization remain in business, but even making profits by attracting more clients due to its competitive pricing policies. It is also important to note here that some projects are helper projects, with limited if any business value considered alone, but necessary for the implementation of other projects, which latter may even become unviable if decoupled of the former. This implies the need for some healthcare organizations to examine carefully the interactions of among projects in their portfolio of ICT projects vis-à-vis other strategies in developing their financial models, to deepen management's perspectives on the overall effects of the various initiatives on the organization and to ensure that they dovetail toward the realization of its strategic business objectives.

The sources of the business value of ICT are legion, but estimating such value is much more than that of the IT project s useful life, or calculating implementation to maintenance costs ratios, or computing net present value of costs and benefits, in a bid to arrive at the project s returns on investment (ROI) for example. Customarily, ROI, the industry standard for determining the feasibility of any new investment or business venture has, with regard ICT investments, mostly cost-based, and technology focused, but it is also important to examine business and performance goals. Indeed, particularly in the healthcare industry, several other factors come into play in determining ROI and the business value of ICT. Hence, it is possible to conceptualize business value of ICT in many ways. However, regardless of how viewed, it is important to base the value of health ICT on its effects on the healthcare organization s business performance, which of course requires consideration of the underlying processes, workflows, decisions, structures, and mechanisms that the ICT would not only change, but probably in positive ways. It is also important to consider both the tangible and intangible effects implemented ICT has on the healthcare organization, and issues relating to ownership by end users, which are anything but trivial in determining business value. Measuring these disparate effects, however, often proves difficult. One could view the business value of ICT in terms of the stakeholders involved, which would make the dimensions of value for a publicly funded healthcare organization quite different from those of a private healthcare provider. One could also adopt a functional approach, for example, making the distinction between ICT deployed in non-clinical versus clinical domains, with the tacit, albeit reasonable assumption that not all aspects of value in the latter would be quantifiable. With regard to the former approach, a private healthcare provider would likely be more interested in calculating its profitability and in being able to generate revenue from invested funds. It would likely want to ensure operations derived from the ICT generates net earnings faster than the cost of borrowing the money invested in it, where ROI would be the ratio of net profit (earnings) to totals investments (total debt plus total equity) expressed in percentages. It is important to ascertain if the net profit value is that before or after tax for accurate comparison of ROI figures, say for different technologies. In a large healthcare organization with shareholders, investors often use a variant of this basic or Du Pont formula, the ratio of net income plus (current minus original value) to original value, again expressed in percentages. Private healthcare organizations would perhaps be interested also to measure ROI on specific things such as equity, assets, or sales. A public healthcare organization, on the other hand would likely pay less attention to profitability, and would less likely consider its services as sales, and perhaps more on other ROI measures. On the other hand, its likely concern would be the provision of high quality healthcare, which of course any private healthcare provider should and many would strive to achieve, in addition to profitability. In looking at the functional perspective of the business value of ICT the above characterization of the profit motive or otherwise of the healthcare organization concerned would apply to non-clinical ICT, and belies the complexity, for example, of ROI computation where questions about what it should measure may not be equally easily determinable. The clinical domain also poses challenges, even if the goal of both private and public healthcare organizations of providing quality services coincides. The first question one might ask would be whether the implemented ICT helps improve the quality of service provision. Let us assume that it does. The next questions would likely be at what costs, and does it yield ROI? Then there is the question of both short and long-term costs and benefits of healthcare ICT implementation to the different stakeholders concerned. These stakeholders, purchasers and employers, healthcare providers, individual patients, even the public and society for examples, would probably have different, even often opposing interests regardless of whether they belong to the private, or public health system. Furthermore, the issue of the project's time span complicates the difficulty involved with determining ROI given different stakeholder perspectives, with a healthcare ICT investment that clearly improves the quality of healthcare delivery to patients in the public or private health sector having varying financial implications for different stakeholders. In the private health sector in particular, and even in the public, this difficulty could jeopardize the chances of investing in ICT that has the potential to improve the efficiency and effectiveness of healthcare delivery, hence save costs, or to prevent medical errors for example, or that patients would benefit from in some other ways. Hence the need for a convincing demonstration of the contextual business value of healthcare ICT in order to ensure support for the provision of the necessary funds for its implementation. Indeed, some contend that without a sound business case, such as showing that a health ICT investment increases margins and yields ROI in a specific period, and indeed, stipulating its specific beneficiaries, the private health sector will show less interest in funding the project. Yet, it would be shortsighted to focus just on cost-saving. operational, and tactical benefits of health ICT investments, as many healthcare organizations are wont to do. The business value of proposed ICT should also encompass a long-term, strategic component that envisions and exploits enduring opportunities for value creation, and competitive edge.

Other factors add to the complexity of determining ICT business value in the health sector. Consider the recent prediction of an international group of experts based on an examination of a systematic review of published studies on dementia that they received from a London-based organization, the Alzheimer's Diseases International. In their report published in the December 17, 2005 issue of The Lancet, the experts estimated that 24.3 million people have dementia today, with 4.6 million new cases of dementia every year, predicted the prevalence doubling every twenty years to 81.1 million by 2040. They also predicted a doubling of the prevalence of dementia by 2040 in developed countries such as the United States, but a tripling in China, India, and other countries in south Asia and the western Pacific. There is serious concern among experts that at these rates, Alzheimer's disease and other dementias are looming major public health issues that would likely overwhelm global economy and healthcare systems if ignored. What is the business value of the urgent public health and other measures required to focus on reducing risk factors for cerebral blood vessel damage, for examples, high blood pressure, smoking, diabetes, and cholesterol? Should public health systems invest in the ICT that could help with the health promotion and primary prevention campaigns that could reduce these risks when significant benefits could accrues from reduced morbidity and mortality but when the financial benefits do not materialize until many years later, reducing the investor's chances to achieve them? Thus, there is need to distinguish between business and economic values, even if both stress pecuniary terms. The long-term economic value today's health ICT investment could yield several years down the road that could be just as important, if not more in its impact on a country and our increasingly interdependent world, even global economy, as the shorter-term benefits of ICT initiatives. This example also shows one of the inherent differences in outlook to health ICT investments between public and private health systems. It seems more likely for private healthcare organizations to be keener on short-term returns on investments, whereas it seems more natural for public health systems to embrace the social value and assimilate the costs of such investments that enhance the health and productivity of persons and society. However, there are often underlying cost control and containment, if not sometimes-outright avoidance considerations and trade-offs even with health ICT investments that public health systems are likely to undertake. Thus, there may be sound economic and social value in a government decision to invest in health ICT for a diabetes prevention or smoking cessation campaign, for example, reduced morbidity and disability costs downstream, but not business value, at least in the short term. No doubt, private healthcare providers could also engage in health ICT projects that only have economic and social value. This could be for a variety of reasons, for examples, for humanitarian reasons, to comply with government regulations, as an expression of social responsibility, for altruistic reasons, with public relations in mind, and to resolve personal and professional moral and ethical concerns, among others. Some would argue though that non-financial motives alone are unlikely to trigger health ICT or any quality improvement initiative for that matter on any major scale in the private health sector. On the other hand, it is not impossible to determine the financial benefits of even some non-financially motivated ICT investments, albeit in the long term.

Regardless of whether the healthcare provider operates in the public or private sector, any investment in ICT requires the use of funds, which are necessarily finite, hence warrants judicious disposition. There is also increasing pressure on publicly funded hospitals to make sound financial decisions as expected of the private sector. In the US, for example, not-for-profit hospitals do not have to adopt the standards stipulated by the Sarbanes-Oxley Act (SOX) (2002), passed in part in response to escalating corporate scandals in the US such as the Enron debacle, as for-profit hospitals do, but many are, nonetheless, particularly some standards, such as those that concern conflicts of interests and internal controls. More publicly funded healthcare providers need to follow suit more so as it would not be difficult for hospital board members, many from the private sector, to appreciate the need for financial transparencies and tighter control over financial activities and processes, hence the business value of implementing ICT that would help achieve these objectives. Investors and financial houses would also likely be more inclined to fund projects proposed by healthcare organizations implementing SOX or any such standard, an indication that these healthcare providers are committed to process improvement and qualitative and honest financial management. Indeed, hospitals both in the public and private health sectors are tightening internal controls where contracts with external agencies influence balance sheets, in particular, the supply chain, understandably as supplies costs almost top the hierarchy of hospital expenses. Many hospitals are changing from unwieldy and inefficient paper-based management of all aspects of supply and service contracts, including initiation, execution, monitoring, and enforcement, to a centralized, more efficient, and transparent automated management approach. Using the appropriate technologies, healthcare organizations would discover that tracking supply costs to individual patients up to billing, including markup determination, becomes routine, and error-free, which enhances the chances of entering correct expenses and revenues on the balance sheets down the road. ICT could also help hospitals avoid conflicts of interests in vendor selection for purchasing contracts as SOX demands. Related also is implementing denials management software, which by automating insurance verification, pre-certifications, and authorizations, revealing the sources of claims errors, reducing claims turnaround times, and preventing them and ensuring payers receive correct claims, could save healthcare organizations significant time and money reducing claims denials. In both of these instances, healthcare organizations, public or private, are not only enhancing their chances of securing funding for capital projects, and their operations, they would be investing in ICT that could help them save significantly, from inflated contractual agreements of uncompetitive bidding, and on the administrative costs of unnecessary claims denials for examples. The business value of such investments is also readily measurable. No one would likely dispute the many other benefits derivable from implementing health ICT. Other than in financial management, ICT could also help in ensuring best practices in the clinical arena, for example, evidence-based practice, and clinical decision support. It could facilitate care processes redesign, and improve clinical workflow, thereby improving efficiency and productivity, and saving costs. It is crucial to integrating disparate units of a health organization, even those geographically dispersed, thereby facilitating information sharing and access to critical patient information at the point of care (POC). Healthcare ICT could help reduce medical errors and enhance patient safety, and overall improve the quality of care delivery. The list goes on. These are benefits many of them, cost-saving benefits, which both public and private healthcare providers should covet. Providing financial justifications for their implementation, however, is a different and often difficult matter, more so as healthcare ICT could be expensive. What is more, many hospital CEOs misjudge the costs by typically focusing on hardware and software costs, disregarding or unaware of other, sometimes-hidden expenditures. It is important in addition to the initial capital outlay of ICT implementation for hospital executives also to consider the "total cost of ownership (TCO)", hardware, software, implementation/ transformation, and maintenance of the proposed ICT. Indeed, they may find out that the costs of hardware and software are relatively minor, usually just about a quarter of total costs, implementation, support, and miscellaneous costs respectively, 45%, 25%, and 5%, typically. Hospitals executives also sometimes discountenance the long-term view necessary to determine the overall costs and benefits of health ICT, which experts recommend should be at least seven years, possibly even more, a seven year TCO ranging between 10%-15% of the project s initial costs. It is no doubt important to consider costs in any financial analysis of proposed ICT implementation, not least because of their role in determining profitability in a specific period. However, it is just as important to consider the benefits that minimize, and even prevent expenses downstream soaring, termed cost avoidance, but not necessarily cost savings, as though influences future operations, may have little if any on present ones. Healthcare executives need to consider the real benefits of such costs, including events in the organization that may nullify the benefits accruing from implementing the ICT. An extension of the concept of TCO is that of total value ownership (TVO) [29]. This concept stresses the importance of considering other factors such as the "softer" qualitative benefits of ICT investments, and not just its tangible, measurable costs, even estimated over the project s entire life span. In other words, it is important to determine the merit or otherwise of an ICT investment to consider the total worth or value of the investment, using in turn, determining a metrics set called cost/ benefit categories, assessing the impact of each category, and employing a relative-based value definition involving a formal base case analysis, and of the utilization period. This way, management could determine the incremental value of their ICT investments, hence their overall business value. In addition, this exercise would help management determine the risk levels of planned health ICT investments, hence facilitate decision making as to which investments to pursue or jettison.

An in-depth review of TVO is beyond the scope of this discussion. However, it is pertinent to underscore its importance to ICT investments particularly in the healthcare industry. The first and perhaps the most crucial step in any TVO evaluation is the determination of the cost/ benefit categories. These categories represent stand-alone and ongoing cost drivers, plus any incremental benefits derivable from investing in those drivers, and potential risk factors that could add to overall costs. It would be difficult, if not impossible for management to conduct this exercise without a correct and detailed perspective of the organization s operations vis-à-vis expenses. Take supplies costs for example. Some hospitals assess supplies expenses as a percentage of net patient revenue, effectively excluding their patient population and the procedures that they carry out, making comparative analysis with their competition impossible given the peculiarities of each hospital. The Medicare Case Mix Index (CMI), a reimbursement mechanism, widely used in the industry in the US, helps address this problem, at least to a certain extent. Its defect is in forecasting supply consumption, with say two or more surgical procedures with the same CMI, utilizing not just different supplies but at different rates and overall amounts, with different, sometimes significant, cost implications. Even measuring supply costs per adjusted patient day is not always a correct evaluation of supplies expenses, because its premise that all hospitals have the same length of stay is inherently flawed. Yet, it is important for a hospital to be able to determine relative supplies costs among similar hospitals that carry out similar procedures at identical frequencies in order to compute as accurately as possible its supply needs, hence costs, including considerations of process redesign and possible ICT implementation, to control these costs if necessary. There are technologies that could help achieve this and supply chain management goals, as the example given earlier shows, with the business value of such technologies not only readily measurable, but could provide supply expense metric that would be invaluable in performance evaluation and quality improvement efforts. The example referred to also highlights the importance of process overhaul in enhancing the chances of ICT improving the healthcare organization and influencing its bottom line. In other words, one should not simply purchase health information systems, just for the sake of automating a medical practice or health organization. There is no point in automating defective workflow processes that is asynchronous with a changing practice, for example. Such processes need redesigning and appropriate ICT aligned to business goals in order to improve efficiency and increase the likelihood of positive outcomes of technology investments. The following news story further helps emphasize the point about understanding cost drivers and the benefits of process redesign and process/ IT alignment. On December 17, 2005, The Record, a Stockton, CA, newspaper reported that thousands of pages of private mental health files from San Joaquin County Mental Health Services (CMHS) turned up in public for everyone to see, dumped in a drop-off area at the Newark Group recycling center[30]. County officials arrived at the scene at 4.30pm to collect the documents although none could explain why confidential patient information supposedly secured behind triple-locked doors at the CMHS North California Street offices ended up at a public disposal facility, according to The Record, although its Director admitted that the incident was a catastrophic failure of its system. Do that system and its processes not need redesigning and overhauling? How difficult should it be making a business case for electronic health records (EHR) given the costs, both tangible and intangible, and relatively easy to conjecture, of such catastrophic failure of paper-based health record systems? There is no doubt that it is more likely though that it is an enduring positive transformation of processes by implemented ICT, which would yield business value than a wholesome acquisition of an IT ¨solution¨, not based on an innovative process do over. Indeed, such business value, if sustained may end up being more than the TCO, in the long term. Although, unlike administrative, and financial processes for examples, it is usually more difficult to make business cases for ICT implementation with clinical processes, particularly when most of its obvious benefits lack equally patent economic or business value. Nonetheless, a variety of clinical processes exist for which making a business case is not necessarily a chore, and it should not be difficult for each functional unit to identify such processes, particularly after a thorough review its processes, and to decide which ones needs more urgent attention. One hospital may decide to redesign its supply chain, as the hypothetical scenario described earlier shows. Another may seek more cost-effective means of medication selection, and usage, in its overall efforts to improve patient safety while simultaneously containing medication costs, and to improve physician workflow processes. In addressing these goals, it may choose to design patient safety solutions that cut across different clinical domains, for example, electronic medical records (EMR), document and database management, pharmacy and lab information systems, and computerized physician order entry (CPOE). Such integration would standardize practice, reduce medical error rates, medication costs, rates of unwarranted lab tests, and hospital stays, and improve patient safety, and scheduling, among others, and are measurable in financial terms. To illustrate this important point, consider the findings of a 2003, cost-benefit analysis of electronic medical records utilization by primary care physicians in an ambulatory setting in the US. This analysis revealed a 5-year net benefit per provider of US$86,400, the results of a five-way sensitivity analysis with the most pessimistic and optimistic assumptions, ranging from a US$2300 net cost to a US$330,900 net benefit. Healthcare providers could save substantially, even amass revenues, from the averted costs of paper charts pulls, re-filings, and transcriptions and governments much more from deploying electronic health records (EHR.) Computerized physician order entry (CPOE) alone, in addition to ensuring patient safety, reducing medical errors, according to some studies by over 50%, flagging redundant laboratory tests, and offering options for less expensive drugs, saved Brigham and Women's Hospital, in Boston, Mass., upwards of $10 million, since it went live on October 07, 2002. A 2001, Health and Health Networks report showed that the 'most wired' hospitals and health organizations had better control of their expenses, had higher credit ratings, improved productivity, and more efficient usage management[23]. In other words, these hospitals performed better than those that had not implemented healthcare ICT.

Canada, with most of its health expenditures spent on hospitals and drugs could save substantially if its hospitals implemented CPOE, not mention the many lives this could save and the improvement in care delivery that would ensue. As previously noted, not only the clinical domains benefit from health ICT implementation, other components of the health sector also do, as clearly revealed in the November 2001 report of a task Force on supply chain management initiated jointly by the Ontario Hospital Association (OHA) and the Efficient Healthcare Consumer Response (EHCR). According to this report, it costs Ontario hospitals approximately $250 million annually to handle and process Ontario s health care supplies, which implementing supply chain

IT and best practices could reduce at least by 15%, or about $40 million. Additionally, the report noted that implementing best practices would reduce overall costs of supplies by a minimum of 5%, or $80 million, a total savings to Ontario hospitals of about $120 million annually, and considering that Ontario is about a third of the Canadian market, an estimated total annual savings across Canada of about $350 million. Even back in the 1970s, studies[31] such as those conducted at the acute care unit at El Camino Hospital and the ambulatory care unit at Harvard Community Health Plan had confirmed the cost saving and quality enhancing values of the transactional information systems, which some hospitals, albeit few compared to the present, had implemented at the time. There is little doubt that a careful, yet comprehensive evaluation of the opportunities clinical processes present for implementing health ICT to improve them, and redesigning these processes to meet targeted goals and subsequently making the right choices on healthcare ICT implementation, will make it easier to build a solid business case for the proposed ICT project. However, it is also important to put all relevant financial parameters in perspective in order to better estimate the prospects or otherwise of the project yielding returns on investments. Equally important is to remember that ICT needs people to create real value, hence the need for financial analyses of health ICT investments to incorporate investments in human capital and just the technologies. Such an approach would also recognize the need to invest in ICT with intangible benefits, and not only those with measurable cost-saving potential, the reasons some advocate such methodologies as TVO over ROI in determining the business value of ICT. Some experts point to the need also to examine the implications of ICT implementation for an organization's competitive edge, evolution of new revenue sources, and improved customer relations boosting even existing markets. In other words, that true business value only emanates from a comprehensive evaluation of the effect of the ICT on organization's overall business performance. Each approach to such determination has its merits and flaws, and each healthcare organization would need to decide which or which combination of methodologies to use based on its needs and available resources to conduct these analyses. It is also important to manage the value creating process, without which the chances of not identifying and accounting for anticipated and emergent values, tangible and intangible values, and other benefits accruing from an ICT are potentially real and could compromise the assessment of the project's outcome, making it difficult to determine its success or failure. The possible impact of this failure on securing funding for future ICT projects that could significantly improve aspects of a healthcare organization's processes and operations could be devastating. This could deny the organization the prospects of added revenues, and of profitability, and the achievement of its business objectives. Perhaps most importantly, it could also threaten its very survival.

Conclusions

There is little doubt that the debate over public and private health systems in Canada will continue. There would be those that continue to see a dichotomy in healthcare delivery, leaning to the public or private model of healthcare delivery, their stance on public and private healthcare financing categorical. The question however, concerns the validity of these diametrically opposed positions in the prevailing socio-political and economic realities in the country. In other words, given the country's history, culture, and institutions, juxtaposed with its geopolitical commitments, and its micro-and macro-economic stations, vis-à-vis an increasingly global economy, what are its options? How could the country attempt to meet the expectations of the country's citizenry for a publicly funded healthcare, or for that matter, those of the seeming contemporary economic imperative of applying free market principles to healthcare delivery? Is the need for reform implicit in the recent Supreme Court ruling in Chaoulli v. Quebec? Is what Canada needs a sort of private/ public health model? If so, what should be its form? Many European countries operate a mixture of public and private health system financing to varying degrees of success. Some had full-blown private health systems side by side their publicly funded systems. Others introduced internal markets to generate competition among healthcare providers. Besides over-bureaucratization, with implications for increasing healthcare costs and compromised equity, there has also been the need in many of these countries, with private health funding added to preexisting public health systems, for more government regulation, which is counter to free-market principles. In the UK, for example, the government has had to establish several "re-regulation" public agencies for insurers and physicians. Added to over-regulation being not in keeping with the concept of free market, in Canada, there is the jurisdictional issue with health service provision being essentially in the provincial/ territorial domain. There is also a good chance of the involvement of private funds from across the Canadian border, further complicating the regulatory measures the Canadian government might be contemplating, which begs the question of the availability or otherwise of the required policy and legal instruments to effect such regulations in this new dispensation. Indeed, it is important for government to start examining the policy implications of the various dimensions of an added private health financing in a milieu of established public health financing, lest caught flat-footed if indeed, the transition to a mix of public and private health financing eventually materializes countrywide. Canada has much to learn from the experiences of the European countries, and those of even far away, Australia, whose experience with private health funding indicates that, the prospects for cost savings through a new or broadened parallel private sector is not substantial, and it hardly reduced its wait times. The country also found that both the private and public health system necessarily interact, albeit in very intricate ways, and regulating private insurers to pursue public objectives, dreadful, which underscores the need for clear health financing policy objectives within which framework public and private health systems must operate. Canada would certainly have to consider the experiences of these different countries, but take its own decisions considering even more its own circumstances within which it ought to situate those vital decisions. Clearly, quality is a major driver of the public/ private health dynamics, and healthcare ICT is central in determining much of the dimensions of quality that would influence the parameters of government policy reforms on health necessary to the implement change and regulate the market if a public/private health-finance mix ultimately emerged.

References:

1. Available at: http://www.healthcoalition.ca/lewis-cma.pdf#search='cma%20ipsosreid%20%20private%20health%20care%20system'
Accessed on November 09, 2005

2. Available at: http://www.canadiandemocraticmovement.ca/displayarticle664.html
Accessed on November 09, 2005

3. Available at:
http://www.canada.com/montreal/montrealgazette/news/editorial/story.html?id=f14-54766-83ba-42a1-a350-962bd65702a8
Accessed on November 11, 2005

4. Available at: http://www.unitednorthamerica.org/phpBB2/about1605.html
Accessed on November 11, 2005

5. Available at:
http://www.ctv.ca/servlet/ArticleNews/story/CTVNews/1080300210232_133?hub=Canada
Accessed on November 11, 2005

6. Available at:
http://www.theglobeandmail.com/servlet/story/RTGAM.20051018.wxparliament18/BNStory/National/
Accessed on November 11, 2005

7. Available at:
http://www.hc-sc.gc.ca/hcs-sss/medi-assur/fedrole/cha-lcs/overview-apercu_e.html
Accessed on November 06, 2005

8. Available at: www.ipsos.ca
Accessed on November 10, 2005

9. Available at:
http://www.conferenceboard.ca/press/documents/FutureHealth.pdf#search='Canada%27s%20health%20expenditures%20over%20the%20years'
Accessed on November 12, 2005

10. Available at:
http://www.dh.gov.uk/PolicyAndGuidance/ResearchAndDevelopment/ResearchAndDevelopmentAZ/PromotingImplementationResearchFindings/PromotingImplementationResearchFindingsArticle/fs/en?CONTENT_ID=4002232&chk=zMUlMn
Accessed on November 13, 2005

11. Available at:
http://www.brighamandwomens.org/gms/News/WangEMRCostBenefit.pdf
Accessed on November 13, 2005

12. Available at: http://www.brighamandwomens.org/feature_july04.asp
Accessed on November 13, 2005

13. Available at:
http://www.oha.com/oha/reports.nsf/($Att)/pspr55mpng/$FILE/SupplyChainManagement.pdf?OpenElement
Accesses on November 13, 2005

14. Greengross, P., Grant, K., and Collini, E., *The U.K National Health Service* 1948 - 1999, Second Edition, Revised July 1999.

15. NHS Management Inquiry (1983,) the Griffiths Report: Letter to the Secretary of State

16. Christenson, CM. Bohmer, R., and Kenagy, J., Will Disruptive Innovations Cure Health Care? Harvard Business Review, Jan/Feb. 1995.
Available at:
http://harvardbusinessonline.hbsp.harvard.edu/b01/en/common/viewFileNavBean.jhtml?_requestid=32822

17. Available at:
http://www.theglobeandmail.com/servlet/story/RTGAM.20051205.wxndp05/BNStory/National/

18. Maccoby M. The Productive Narcissist: The Promise and Peril of Visionary Leadership NY, USA: Broadway Books, 2003

19. Available at: http://www.meridianbooster.com/story.php?id=200121
Accessed on December 6, 2005

20. National Health Expenditure Trends, 1975-2001
Available at: http://secure.cihi.ca/cihiweb/dispPage.jsp?cw_page=spend_e
Accessed on: December 6, 2005

21. Statistics Canada, Health Indicators, 2005

22. Health Canada, EBIC, 1998

23. Solovy, A, The Big payback, *Hospital and Networks*, July 2001

24. Available at:
http://www.thestar.com/NASApp/cs/ContentServer?pagename=thestar/Layout/Article_Type1&c=Article&cid=1133995815308&call_pageid=968332188774&col=968350116467 Accessed on December 8, 2005

25. IOM 1998: Statement on Quality of Care, National Roundtable on Health Care Quality
Available at: http://www.nap.edu/catalog/9439.html

Accessed on December 8, 2005

26. IOM 2001: Crossing the Quality Chasm: A New Health System for the 21st Century
Available at: http://www.iom.edu/object.file/master/27/184/0.pdf
Accessed on December 8, 2005

27 IOM 1999: To Err is Human: Building A Safer Health System
Available at: http://www.iom.edu/Object.File/Master/4/117/0.pdf

28. Available at: http://www.leapfroggroup.org/news/leapfrog_news/1171443
Accessed on December 8, 2005

29. Dempsey. J Dvorak, RE., Holen, E., et. al: A hard and soft look at IT investment. The McKinsey Quarterly 1998 1: 126-137

30. Available at:
http://www.recordnet.com/apps/pbcs.dll/article?AID=/20051217/NEWS01/512170380/1001/NEWS01
Accessed on December 18, 2005

31. Office of Technology Assessment 1977, Policy Implications of Medical Information Systems, Washington DC

December 24, 2005

www.ingramcontent.com/pod-product-compliance
Lightning Source LLC
Chambersburg PA
CBHW020616220526
45463CB00006B/2598